The Cowichan

Duncan, Chemainus, Ladysmith and Region

The Cowichan

DUNCAN, CHEMAINUS, LADYSMITH AND REGION

Including Cobble Hill, Cowichan Bay, Cowichan Lake and communities,

Crofton, Glenora, Maple Bay, Mill Bay and Shawnigan Lake

GEORGINA MONTGOMERY

photography by KEVIN OKE

HARBOUR PUBLISHING

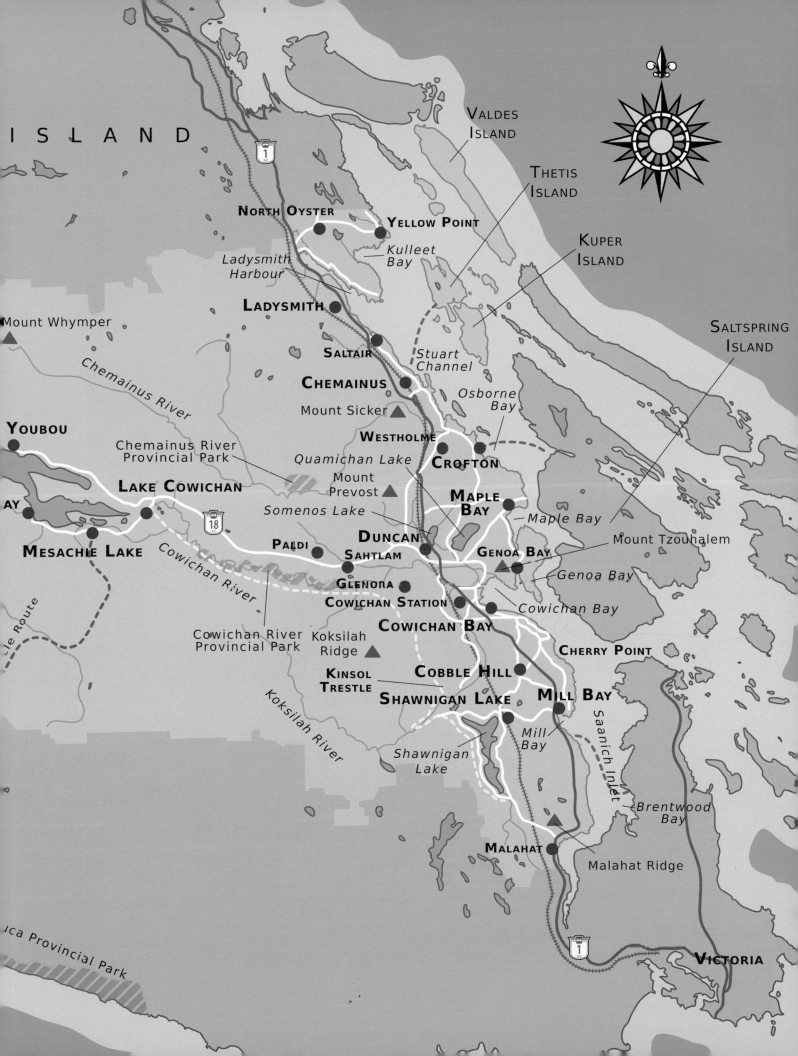

A fisherman in action along the legendary Cowichan River.

Page 1: Emily Sawyer-Smith knits Cowichan sweaters for Hill's Native Art south of Duncan.

Page 2–3: Early morning on a Cowichan estuary farm.

Contents

1

Postcard from the Cowichan

It's the sublime beauty of the Cowichan's landscape—more accurately, its many landscapes—that first strikes a visitor. How could so much natural beauty be in one place?

The region's long east coast is a succession of broad bays, narrow coves, deep inlets, rocky shores, sculpted sandstone ledges, soft sand beaches and small islands. Inland, its broad river valleys cradle sweeping green fields, forested slopes, and rivers, wetlands and lakes of all size. Mountains crowd its interior, eventually giving way in the west to moist rainforested valleys and a rugged coastline fronting the Pacific Ocean. In the Cowichan you can find both prickly pear cactus growing on the dry east coast and massive trees growing on the humid west coast—trees so old that many were seedlings long before Christopher Columbus was born and even long before the time of Genghis Khan.

So many different landscapes also support a wide variety of communities: seaside villages, several with views to the mainland's snow-capped mountains; lakeside summer holiday destinations; rural hamlets of farms and vineyards; urban centres filled with heritage buildings, upscale shops and nearly everything a big city offers; new residential developments overlooking the ocean or a lake; and small interior towns that sit on the

Sunrise view from Mount Prevost, looking over Duncan toward the southern Gulf Islands.

doorstep of a backcountry full of hiking, camping and other outdoor recreation opportunities.

In between the communities on the eastern side of the region, large dairy farms, hay fields, market gardens, vineyards, alpaca ranches, hobby farms and horse paddocks fan out beyond roadways. Whatever the scene, there always seems to be a high peak or mountain ridge rising just beyond: Koksilah Ridge, Mount Tzouhalem, Mount Prevost, Mount Brenton and others. Inland, around Lake Cowichan, mountain views are the order of the day, and forests more than fields fill the spaces between communities.

"Cowichan Valley" and "Cowichan Region" are not names you'll find on a Geological Survey of Canada map. Nevertheless, these are the most common names you'll hear from people referring to the area of eastern Vancouver Island that lies roughly between the Malahat Ridge in the south, Nanaimo in the north, and inland west to Cowichan Lake. What you will find on a map are four place names containing the word Cowichan—lake, river, estuary and bay—a clearly connected series of physical features that accounts in many ways for how the region has come to be called.

Notionally, however, and administratively since 1967, there's much more to the Cowichan than even the local government's name, the Cowichan Valley Regional District, suggests. In fact the district boundaries extend not only from the top of the Malahat to just beyond Ladysmith in the north, but also offshore to include the small Gulf Islands of Valdes, Thetis and Kuper along Vancouver Island's east coast. Then heading inland, the boundaries wow out in a generous swath that runs all the way to the island's west coast. This takes in Shawnigan and Cowichan Lakes, the Cowichan, Chemainus and Koksilah valleys, the Carmanah and

The Cowichan

Above: *Native Heritage*, painted in 1983 by Paul Ygartua, was one of the first Chemainus murals. It features notable figures from the region's First Nations past.

Above right: The Quw'utsun' Cultural and Conference Centre, located in Duncan, showcases the culture and history of the Cowichan people.

Walbran valleys and Nitinat Lake, and the south part of Pacific Rim National Park, located along Vancouver Island's west coast.

The district is 3,730 square kilometres (1,440 square miles) in area, roughly twice the size of the Hawaiian island of Maui or six times the size of the city of Toronto. Within it lie the four municipalities of Duncan, North Cowichan, Lake Cowichan and Ladysmith, plus nine electoral districts that include more than a dozen smaller towns, villages and hamlets. Most of the Cowichan's population of more than 80,000 live on the eastern coastal side of the island in communities that have expanded in recent years with an increasing number of young families, Victoria and Nanaimo commuters, and retirees.

Not surprisingly some district residents (those living in the Chemainus River valley, for instance) consider "Cowichan Valley" a woefully narrow and inaccurate name for describing the area overall. It's hard to argue the point once you know the extent of the district and begin to discover the seemingly endless number of valleys and pocket glens folded into its terrain. Cleverly, even the Cowichan Valley Regional District has adopted "Cowichan Region" or simply "Cowichan" to get around the moniker challenge. These names most residents seem happy to accept.

The word Cowichan derives from the Coast Salish *shkewétsen*, which is translated variously as "basking in the sun," "warm back" and "warm country." According to First Nations oral history, the First Peoples living on the Cowichan estuary could see an enormous frog that appeared to be sitting, back to the sun, in the rock face of the mountain now called Tzouhalem. They gave both the mountain and then themselves this name. Over time, *shkewétsen* became Quw'utsun' (also sometimes spelled Khowutzun) and, several more variations later, Cowichan. Also over time "basking in the sun" and the other translations have given way to the now most frequently repeated version, "warm land." It seems an apt description in many ways and not just because of the eastern side's sub-Mediterranean climate.

The benign climate and wealth of natural resources across the entire region have attracted people for millennia. Since before the time of Egypt's Old Kingdom, the First Nations in the Cowichan have been an abiding presence. "Part of the uniqueness of the Cowichan landscape," writes historian Daniel P. Marshall, "is that the Cowichan tribes have inhabited it for thousands upon thousands of years." Most of the region lies in the traditional territory of the

Hul'qumi'num. While only about 10 percent of the region's population today is aboriginal, the First Nations cultural imprint is deep. Cowichan Tribes, an amalgamation of six of the region's First Nations, is the largest single band in BC. It owns and operates several large businesses, including Cherry Point Vineyards in Cobble Hill and the Quw'utsun' Cultural and Conference Centre in Duncan, and it manages numerous commercial properties.

As modern as all of the region's First Nations have become, however, ancient tradition remains a potent unifying force. Private ceremonies such as winter dances still take place in the bighouses, and the Shaker religion is still widely practised. People still gather traditional native plants for ritual and medicinal use, such as the consumption plant (also known as Indian celery) to make a tea to ease the symptoms of a cold. Spearfishing is still carried out along the rivers in the fall. Storytelling, singing, dancing and drumming are still highly valued skills. Carving, weaving, painting and knitting are still honoured arts, though many practitioners experiment with applying modern artistic techniques to traditional forms. Duncan's collection of more than 80 totem poles honours both Cowichan and other First Nations cultures in a highly visible way. And the distinctive Cowichan sweater is, like a hand-rolled Cuban cigar, a regionally unique, individually crafted item that discerning shoppers from around the world seek out when they come to BC.

A young member of the Tzinquaw Dancers. According to legend, Tzinquaw (Thunderbird) rid Cowichan Bay of Quannis (Killer Whale) to protect salmon runs. The story of the bloody battle between the two supernatural beings was dramatized in the internationally acclaimed 1950 opera, *Tzinquaw*, written in Duncan and performed by an all-Cowichan cast.

The Cowichan

Above: Cowichan Tribes owns and operates several large businesses, including Cherry Point Vineyards in Cobble Hill.

Right: A worker at Cherry Point Vineyards.

Opposite top: Cyclists on the Cowichan portion of the Trans Canada Trail.

Opposite bottom: The Cowichan is noted for its large and active equestrian community.

Pages 16–17: Some of the world's largest and oldest trees grow in the Carmanah and Walbran river valleys in the western Cowichan region.

A century and a half ago this area attracted scores of adventurous newcomers—British, continental European, East Indian, Chinese, Japanese and Hawaiian, among others. Many turned up from distant goldfields where, after failing to strike it rich, they came to their senses and flocked instead to the Cowichan's motherlode. Others came to this West Coast frontier to seize whatever opportunities they could; most became farmers, loggers, sawmill workers, coal and copper miners and cannery workers. The result is a region built and shaped by generations of multi-ethnic and multicultural enterprise.

The first settlers arrived by sea, most through Cowichan Bay, Maple Bay and Chemainus. The coming of the E&N Railway in the late 1880s, completed with symbolic spike-driving by Canada's prime minister Sir John A. Macdonald, set a new era into motion for the Cowichan. Agriculture and forestry expanded, towns and villages sprouted up alongside the rail line, and more people arrived from away. A couple of decades later the first highway from Victoria ignited the same kind of burst, exposing the Cowichan's plentiful assets and resources even more.

Today the trend continues. Highway, ferry and airline access makes it easier than ever to travel to and from the Cowichan and to explore its farthest corners. Business and industry have grown within the region, though they have shifted away from the primary resource dependence of the past. Service, professions, agriculture, retail, manufacturing and tourism are now key areas of employment. The region's food and wine industry has also taken root. Culinary enthusiasts, slow-food advocates and others keen to join the already large ranks of small-scale

food growers and producers, are being drawn to the Cowichan's bounty in the same way the first wave of newcomers were.

The region's outdoor recreation options are as renowned as its agricultural riches. Here a person can scuba dive or sail off the island's east coast on one day; play 18 holes of golf, cycle the Trans Canada Trail or swim in a lake the next day; and go backcountry hiking or whitewater kayaking the day after that.

Recreational anglers from around the world were among the first to discover the region's fish-filled waters, coming to the Cowichan in the late 1800s to cast their lines into its soon-to-be legendary lakes and rivers and off its saltwater coast. Hotels and lodges at Lake Cowichan and along the Cowichan River catered to wealthy businessmen, actors, diplomats and royals, Archduke Ferdinand of Austria among the latter. The region is still a fishing destination, but its reputation as an outdoor playground has ballooned as the types of sporting and recreational pursuits have increased and so too the awareness of the Cowichan as a good place to do them. For many the added bonus is being able to go and get wet, dirty and happily thrilled yet still be within easy reach of a hot shower and a cold drink at the end of the day in nearly any of the Cowichan's towns and villages.

The region's many provincial, regional and community parks—in addition to Pacific Rim National Park—let campers, hikers, swimmers and boaters of every skill and comfort level experience the great outdoors in just the dose they want. A particularly Cowichan summer activity is tubing down the Cowichan River—that is, floating (or careening, in high-water conditions) down the river aboard an inflated inner

The Legendary Cowichan River

Geographically and historically, the key feature of the Cowichan region is the legendary Cowichan River. Its praises have been sung in sporting clubs, tackle shops and fishing magazines around the world for over a century. Stories are still told of how, in the 1920s, angling clubs in New York received weekly bulletins reporting fishing conditions on the Cowichan River. Today's anglers still consider the Cowichan to be one of the finest trout streams in BC. Seven species of game fish have kept the Cowichan on the map as a fishing destination of choice: coho, chinook and chum salmon and steelhead, rainbow, brown and cutthroat trout.

From its start at Cowichan Lake, the river sweeps 47 kilometres (29 miles) through gorges, 130 sets of rapids and 30 sets of falls before emptying into Cowichan Bay. Along the way other smaller streams and creeks (such as those flowing out of Quamichan and Somenos Lakes) join with the river as it nears sea level.

In 2004 the river received Canadian heritage river status, making it only the third river in BC (after the Fraser and Kicking Horse) to gain that recognition. Based on its exceptional natural, cultural and recreational values, it had already received a provincial heritage river

The Cowichan River received Canadian heritage river status in 2004 in recognition of its outstanding natural, cultural and recreational values.

designation in 1995, plus protection in long stretches as the Cowichan River Provincial Park. In the summer the Cowichan is hugely popular for swimming, boating and tubing.

The river and its estuary were central to the existence of First Nations for several millennia. Even today spearfishing along the riverbanks during the fall remains a tradition. The fish hatchery on the river is operated by the Department of Fisheries and Oceans in co-operation with Cowichan Tribes. Settlers arriving in the late 1800s were quick to appreciate the river too. The rich alluvial soils blanketing the valley bottom made farming not only possible but profitable. And a robust system of dikes helped rein in the helter-skelter channels of the river's lower reaches.

In recent years declining stocks of some fish, notably chinook and coho salmon, have raised concerns over the river's health, but many parties—from government and small business to conservation groups and sport-fishing interests—are on alert. Restocking efforts and work to repair and protect the river environment are under way.

Above: A paraglider in flight from the top of Mount Prevost.

Left: The Islands Folk Festival, which takes place at the end of July at Providence Farm, is the second-oldest folk festival in the province.

tube from an oversized truck tire. Diehard windsurfing and kiteboarding devotees head to the Cowichan's tidal Nitinat Lake, voted by aficionados as one of North America's top boarding destinations. Paragliders set sail off the sheer cliff face of Mount Prevost, riding the updrafts high above the valley floor. And mountain bikers gather regularly from all parts of the island to attack, grind and bunny-hop their way up, over and down the region's hundreds of kilometres of trails.

Horseback riding and rowing are also seriously pursued in the Cowichan, both having a long history in the area. Annual equestrian events bring participants and competitors to the region throughout the year, as do rowing events involving many of the local public and private schools. Brentwood College and Shawnigan Lake School host the largest rowing regattas. Meanwhile, local and international court action carries on as always at the century-old South Cowichan Lawn Tennis Club in Cowichan Bay, said to be the world's second-oldest lawn tennis club after Wimbledon.

The many artists and artisans who call the Cowichan home are outnumbered only by their admiring public, the supportive arts communities that exist across the region. Two large professional theatre venues plus at least half a dozen other smaller facilities stage live theatre, symphony, ballet and other performing arts year-round. There's also a hopping live music scene (regularly booking jazz, blues, classical, choral, folk, Celtic, country and bluegrass performers), numerous museums and art galleries, and two unusual art collections: the totems in Duncan and more than 50 outdoor murals and sculptures in Chemainus. Annual arts and cultural competitions, festivals and special events enjoy large attendance by local residents and out-of-towners alike.

All of this together adds up to a place that's as exquisitely diverse in character as it is beautiful in setting.

2

The Cowichan Stage

The setting of the Cowichan's stage began with hundreds of millions of years of tectonic plate activity, volcanic action, erosion and glaciation. Once the ice sheets retreated some 12,000 years ago, leaving a scoured landscape and deep deposits of glacial till, the area's two great rivers—the Cowichan and the Chemainus—got to work channel cutting and estuary building. And as occurred elsewhere on the warming continent, plant and animal life returned.

Most of the region lies on Vancouver Island's lee side, away from the high winds and storms off the Pacific Ocean. Lying in the rain shadow of the Olympic Mountains located in Washington State to the south also affords the Cowichan some precipitation relief. The region claims the highest average mean temperature in Canada, 11°C (51.8°F). The summertime temperature averaged across the region is 23°C (73.4°F) and from December to January is 5.6°C (42.1°F), though the tremendous variety in terrain in this one small region

A view west over Cowichan Lake's North Arm. The road skirting the lake on the north side leads to the town of Youbou.

means there is considerable variety in temperature and climate between areas.

The low-elevation east side of the region, lying in the West Coast's sub-Mediterranean climate zone, enjoys the moderating effects of the Strait of Georgia, often referred to as an "inland sea." Sunny, warm summers and mild winters are the norm. In most communities along this coast, sailing, cycling and hiking continue year-round, and many people dine from winter gardens.

Up in the mountainous interior of the region, the climate rapidly shifts to maritime. Cowichan Lake, which lies about 162 metres (530 feet) above sea level, receives on average more than twice the amount of annual precipitation, including snowfall, than the Duncan area does. Snow hangs on late into the spring atop mountain peaks, many of which reach well over 1,000 metres (3,280 feet). On the other hand, summer temperatures around the lake are generally higher than on either coast. Over on the far west side of the region, in the Carmanah and Walbran valleys and down to the Pacific, the climate is mild and wet year-round, offering perfect growing conditions for the lush coastal rainforests that thrive here. The amount of annual rainfall in this part of the Cowichan averages about 300 centimetres (120 inches), or four times what the east side of the region receives.

Top: The arbutus tree thrives in dry coastal areas of the eastern Cowichan.

Below: A snowy scene in an inland area of the Cowichan.

With two very different coastal environments—one relatively dry, the other relatively wet and humid—plus a large, high-elevation interior area, the Cowichan has a tremendous variety and abundance of plant life. Most forests of the region's east coast are a mix of coniferous and deciduous trees, mainly second-growth Douglas fir, bigleaf maples and red alder. On dry rocky slopes, the West Coast's distinctive evergreen deciduous tree, the arbutus, stands out.

Away from the shore, other tree species characteristic of the area appear, including Pacific dogwood, western flowering dogwood and Garry oak (whose range, like the arbutus, is extremely limited in southwestern BC). The forests in the interior and west to the rainforests of the Pacific side of the region are renowned for their stands of massive old trees. Western red cedar, yellow cedar, Douglas fir, Sitka spruce, western hemlock and others make up this "giant class" of towering, large-diameter, millennium-aged trees.

Across the region, hundreds of species of flowers, ferns, mosses, grasses and shrubs flourish. Salal, salmonberry and vanilla leaf abound. In the spring, forest floors declare the end of winter with a show of trilliums, fairy slippers (often referred to as calypso orchids), shooting stars and several species of *Erythronium* or fawn lilies. Meanwhile, deep blue camas and perky yellow buttercups fill Garry oak meadows, and voluptuous green and yellow skunk cabbages unfold in bogs and marshes. In alpine meadows in the region's interior mountains, more than 40 species of flowers bloom from May through July. In the fall, forest floors yield a profusion of mushrooms, including many edible species (such as the much-coveted chanterelle) that become the object of intense desire by recreational fungi foragers.

The region's two large estuaries draw great numbers of year-round and migratory water birds. In the winter, it's common to see large flocks of trumpeter swans on both estuaries and on inland fields, vivid white against the green. Their *connhk-connhk* call as they fly in V-formations from estuary to field and back again is an annual Cowichan sound. Bald eagles, large black raptors with white hoods and tails, are also common in the region. In the fall, they collect along the rivers to feed on the wild coho, chinook and chum salmon that return from the ocean to spawn and die in the same river in which they were born. Great blue herons are

Above: Hundreds of species of mushrooms grow in Cowichan forests. Among the edible varieties is the prized golden chanterelle.

Below: During the winter, Somenos marsh (shown here) and Somenos Lake are home to thousands of waterfowl, including an estimated five percent of the world's trumpeter swan population.

found all along the coast. Cowichan Bay has one of Vancouver Island's largest heron colonies. A small sample of other birds native to the region includes turkey vultures, pileated woodpeckers, quail, Steller's jays, ravens, kingfishers, hummingbirds and grouse.

As well as salmon, the Cowichan's large rivers contain kokanee, Dolly Varden char and several types of trout. Notable land mammals in the region include red squirrels, blacktail deer, Roosevelt elk (the largest elk subspecies in North America), cougars and black bears. Marine life visible from coastal beaches and parks ranges from vast numbers and species of shore birds to otters, harbour seals and Steller's and California sea lions. Orcas frequent the Gulf Island waters off eastern Vancouver Island, and grey whales pass along the Pacific side of the island in the spring and fall on their annual migration. In intertidal zones, under shoreline rocks and attached to dock pilings lives a whole other world of plant and animal life, from bright green eelgrass and kelp to jellyfish, tube worms, anemones, crabs and purple and red sea stars.

It was to this natural bounty on land and in local waters that the region's first inhabitants arrived.

The People Who Fell from the Sky

The first people to step onto the Cowichan stage are believed to have started arriving at least 5,000 years ago. Dozens of archeological sites in the region have yielded evidence of ancient habitation.

Springtime show: a western trillium surrounded by uncurling fiddleheads.

According to First Nations oral history, twelve people were dispatched from the sky to the virginal wilderness of earth below. Syalutsa was first, falling near what is now called Koksilah Ridge. He was followed by his younger brother Stutsun, who landed between the two peaks of Swuqus, the commanding landmark northwest of Duncan now named Mount Prevost. Others fell to Skw'aakw'nus (Mount Sicker), Pulumutsun (Mount Brenton), the mouth of the Chemainus River and Puneluxutth' (Penelakut Spit). From these individuals and the others who followed, the Cowichan Tribes originated.

However, in a turn of events recounted by first cultures, a great flood nearly wiped out these

early residents. Syalutsa, alerted to the coming devastation, carved a large canoe. Then he wove a very long rope and attached one end to the canoe. He climbed Swuqus and secured the other end of the rope to the enormous boulder that still sits atop the mountain today. With the boat safely anchored, Syalutsa got aboard and rode out the flood. Nearly everyone else in the region died. He might have stayed a lonely man had good fortune not intervened. Several months after the waters receded, the chief of the nearby T'Sou-ke tribe, another human who had fallen from the sky and survived the flood, got word of Syalutsa being alive. He sent his daughter Teyqumut to find him, which she did. Initial misunderstandings almost thwarted their relationship, but finally the couple united and the repopulating of the Cowichan Tribes began.

So powerful did the Cowichan people become that in 1808, when Simon Fraser reached the mouth of what was later named the Fraser River, local Natives warned him of the fierce "Ka-way-chin" who ruled much of the territory between the mainland river and the ocean.

Most of today's Cowichan region lies in the traditional territory of the Coast Salish ethnic group known as the Hul'qumi'num. The group's traditional language also goes by that name. Group members in the region are the Cowichan, Chemainus, Penelakut, Lyackson, Halalt and Lake Cowichan Nations. The southern end of the Cowichan Valley Regional District lies within the traditional territory of the Malahat First Nation. The western part of the region, from Lake Cowichan to the west coast of Vancouver Island, lies within Ditidaht territory.

The Cowichans are thought to have been the largest tribe on North America's west coast in the early 1800s, with an estimated 5,000 members. Most people lived in seven villages on the Cowichan estuary and lower reaches of the river: Xwulqw'selu (Koksilah), S'amuna' (Somena), Qw'umiyiqun (Comiaken), Xinupsum (Kneipsen), Kw'amutsun (Quamichan), Lhumlumluts (Clem Clemluts) and Tl'ulpalus (Kilpalas).

Regardless of the might and wealth of the Cowichan people, one force undermined them. The once powerful nation was nearly wiped out by the arrival of the Europeans and their smallpox, firearms and alcohol. By 1912 the Cowichan Nation's population had fallen to about 500.

However, the resilience of the Cowichan people, and indeed of all First Nations in the region, deeply colours the spirit of the place today. "When you consider," says historian

Quamichan village scene, c. 1880s, with Mount Tzouhalem in the background.
BC Archives D-00692

Fish weirs, like this recent one installed on the Cowichan River, were commonly used by First Nations. The temporary fence-like structures prevent migrating salmon from getting past, making them easier to capture.

The Cowichan

Tzouhalem, the Cowichan's Mighty Warrior

Tzouhalem is one of the best-remembered figures of recent Cowichan history. Some would say he was a violent and unscrupulous man interested only in looking after his own interests. Others would say he was a bold and aggressive defender of aboriginal rights. In all likelihood, the Cowichan warrior was a potent blend of both characterizations.

Born in the early 1800s, Tzouhalem was said to have been an ugly child with a large head and a small body. He compensated for his physical weaknesses by becoming as fierce a fighter as the Cowichan people ever produced. Tzouhalem thought nothing of killing rivals and taking their widows for himself—a technique that landed him more than 40 wives during his life.

In 1844 Tzouhalem, resentful of the European newcomers' intrusion into his people's territory, tried to capture the Hudson's Bay Company fort at present-day Victoria. He and his small band of warriors did not succeed. On top of that, when he returned home to the Cowichan, Tzouhalem found that even his own people had by then become fed up with him and his devious, troublemaking ways. They banished Tzouhalem from the villages. With several of his young followers, he moved into a cave on the mountain that now bears his name beside Cowichan Bay.

In a classic case of never knowing when to quit, Tzouhalem met his end on Kuper Island in 1859 while trying to make off with yet another man's wife. The mountain of Shkewétsen (Khowutzun) was later renamed Tzouhalem by First Nations in recognition of the warrior.

A totem pole at the Quw'utsun' Cultural and Conference Centre in Duncan features the 19th-century warrior Tzouhalem.

Daniel P. Marshall, this "extended and continuous habitation . . . about 25 times the age of the European presence, . . . it is then that one begins to finally realize the incredible permanence of the Cowichan peoples."

The People Who Arrived by Sea

Next to wander onto the Cowichan stage were the Europeans. Some historians believe that the English circumnavigator Sir Francis Drake sailed by eastern Vancouver Island as early as 1579. Other historical evidence suggests that in 1592 the Cowichan was visited by Juan de Fuca, who is known to have piloted a Spanish ship that year on an undocumented trip around the southern tip of Vancouver Island. A later Spanish sailing expedition made its way up the Strait of Georgia in 1791. Eventually, however, it was the British who arrived in force on this part of the island starting in the early 1800s and decided to stay.

Between 1824 and 1827, Hudson's Bay Company trader John Work travelled in the area and in his journals mentioned the "Coweechin River." Among the usual actors to follow such a reconnaissance were missionaries, government agents and prospectors. Attempts at more permanent settlements gradually began in the mid-1850s.

A pivotal moment in the Cowichan's development occurred when governor of Vancouver Island, James Douglas, escorted 78 settlers aboard the HMS *Hecate* to Cowichan Bay in August 1862. The newcomers, given access to over 18,000 hectares (45,000 acres) of arable land, dug in.

Another defining moment in the Cowichan's development was the building of the Esquimalt and Nanaimo (E&N) Railway. In 1881 the British Columbia government asked Victoria businessman Robert Dunsmuir to build a rail line up the island. In return for taking the project on, Dunsmuir received 809,400 hectares (2 million acres) on the island and $750,000 of federal funds. Three years later on August 13, 1886, Prime Minister Sir John A. Macdonald, travelling aboard Dunsmuir's private railway car, *Maude,* arrived at Cliffside on the east side of Shawnigan Lake. There Macdonald applied silver mallet to golden spike, ceremonially completing the line. The party then continued north with a few more stops, including the one that garnered Duncan its own station (see chapter four).

The E&N went into operation in 1887, creating a boom in the overland transport of farm and forest products and opening up further areas of the Cowichan to development. Passenger rail service also took off, though not everyone approved. Train historian Robert D. Turner writes, "Despite the annoyance of Victoria's clergy, E&N trains ran on Sundays. Dunsmuir is reported to have commented that he considered it a public benefit since it took those who did not attend church from the cities and removed them from evil influences."

After Dunsmuir died in 1905, his son James sold the E&N and adjacent lands to Canadian Pacific Railway, which kept and operated the line until 1999.

Moss thrives in the Cowichan's rainforests.

The World Comes to the Cowichan

For newcomers to the Cowichan today, much of the region's attraction is its air of having stayed sheltered from the wider world. Appearances, of course, can be deceiving, as Kathryn Gagnon, curator of the Cowichan Valley Museum and Archives based in Duncan, will attest. Kathryn, who took over the reins from long-time curator Priscilla Lowe in 2004, knew this part of Vancouver Island a little before moving to it to take up her new position, but it was only after being on the job for a few months that she realized the extent of the Cowichan's many links with world events.

"A person might come to a small, quiet corner of the country like this, thinking it's probably rather insulated in some ways," she says, "but you quickly find out how wrong a notion that is. I've been constantly amazed in discovering how many connections Cowichan has had in the last 150 years with other places, people and events around the globe."

Peeling back the layers of the Cowichan reveals what Kathyrn means.

The E&N passenger train crossing the Cowichan River at Duncan, c. 1890.
BC Archives A-09730

With the arrival of the train, economic opportunities in agriculture, mining, forestry and fishing swelled and so did the influx of immigrants. Hard-working labourers seeking a better life, they arrived in the Cowichan from all over the world including the British Isles, the US, every country in continental Europe and Scandinavia, India, China, Japan and the Hawaiian Islands. The nature of life in the newly forming communities was such that everyone—

regardless of nationality or ethnic or religious background—was generally in the same boat, sweating it out alongside each other to cobble together a life in the New World or to send money back home. Working in the fields, forests, mines or canneries, and with a shared background of humble means, the majority of immigrants to the Cowichan developed a generally co-operative, shoulder-to-shoulder attitude to their dealings with each other.

In remote forestry camps, workers slept in rustic bunkhouses or in tents, eating together in cookhouses and putting in long days that turned into long weeks of dangerous and physically taxing work. Loggers also often faced several hours of commuting between camp and the area they were cutting. At longer-established camps, whole families sometimes moved in, which helped create better-rounded settlements than existed in the single-men-only camps. Around Cowichan Lake, early logging camps weren't even built on land. All the structures—sleeping quarters, cookhouse, storage sheds, office, connecting walkways—were built on floats and rafted together. Secured to shore, they provided easy land access, but they were ready for towing to another part of the lake in pursuit of the wood supply.

Compared with their forestry brethren, miners, such as those working in the coal mines north and west of Ladysmith and in Mount Sicker's copper mines, spent a less nomadic life and worked relatively close to where they lived.

However, all the one-to-one co-operation didn't stop ethnic and cultural enclaves from forming. Hardly had Ladysmith's new residents unpacked their bags, for example, than a Finn Town, Belgian Town and Little Italy materialized. All groups mixed out of necessity in coping with everyday life, but often kept to themselves when it came to socializing. Discrimination along racial boundaries also developed, but was most clearly directed at Chinese workers, a group that had been coming to the country in great number since the mid-1800s. Most of these immigrants arrived alone, partly because of the costly $500 head tax (in 1904) that Canada forced each Chinese newcomer to pay. Few could afford to bring their families too. No surprise, then, that a subclass emerged in all communities in the region's early days. Richard Goodacre writes in his book *Dunsmuir's Dream: Ladysmith—The First Fifty Years*, "Unlike the European immigrant, the Chinese in this period did not come to stay, and did not put down roots. They lived in separate communities of single men, isolated by race, language, custom, and prejudice."

Unlikely loggers posing on springboards and holding a crosscut saw at the base of a notched Douglas fir, c. 1906.
Cowichan Valley Museum
1987.5.3.9.2

The Longstocking Years

A notable period for the Cowichan started with the great flock of British upper-crust immigrants who began swanning into the region in the late 1800s. Finding it much to their liking, they quickly set about building country estates, laying out cricket pitches and planning fancy-dress parties. So many were former officers of the British Indian Army that the term "longstocking," referring to the puttees and shorts the officers wore in exotic colonial postings, soon became a catch-all phrase for anyone with a British background and financial means.

The ripples from the Longstockings' landing touched nearly every facet of life in the region, from education and recreation to politics and the economy. Even Samuel Maclure, the noted residential architect of the time in BC, became a Longstocking favourite. Several homes built in the Cowichan area during that period took on Maclure's signature "bungalow" features, such as half-timbered and fieldstone masonry exteriors, high pitched roofs, porches and

Fairbridge Farm School

The Fairbridge Drive neighbourhood just south of Duncan contains remnants of the 405-hectare (1,000-acre) Prince of Wales Fairbridge Farm School.

Between 1935 and 1949, this became the new home of 329 underprivileged British children sent "out to the colony" for a chance at a better life. Fairbridge Canada was the second in a residential school network created by South African Rhodes scholar Kingsley Fairbridge pursuing his "vision splendid." It was a highly favoured philanthropic cause in its day in England and Canada. Not only the Prince of Wales but other royals, government, big business, socialites, average citizens and not-so-average citizens (such as Rudyard Kipling) rushed forward to be its patrons. Within a few years the farm school had expanded to 27 buildings, including dormitories, principal's residence, dining hall and cook's cottage, large day school, gymnasium and library, hospital, farm buildings and 300-seat chapel. Few of the children ever saw their parents again until adulthood, when many did make visits back to Britain.

Seventeen of the original Fairbridge buildings still stand, most now converted to single-family homes, and the chapel clock still chimes hourly across the commons. Every two years the former students, most now in their 80s, return to visit the place and attend a tea hosted by the street's current residents. One Old Fairbridgian, John Cowans, arrived at the school in 1937 when he was only six years old. John,

Fairbridge Chapel received provincial heritage status in 1988 and is today a popular venue for weddings and musical performances.

who passed away in late 2008 after a life well lived in the Cowichan, once said in an interview about the biennial get-togethers, "When we return to Fairbridge, it's not just a school reunion. It's like a family gathering."

Boys at the Prince of Wales Fairbridge Farm School head off to do chores, 1938. *Cowichan Valley Museum 1997.9.1.11*

grand entrance halls—features reflecting Maclure's love of both the Arts and Crafts and Tudor revival architectural styles. Some of these homes can still be seen in the Cowichan today.

Duncan, as the region's commercial centre, was especially imprinted by this group. For instance, their remittances, stipends, British pension cheques and other financial sources buoyed the community when economic difficulties depressed surrounding areas. Tom Henry, in his book *Small City in a Big Valley: The Story of Duncan*, writes:

> In the Depression of the 1930s, especially, when Longstocking population was at its peak, with more than 400 families and 1,500 individuals, their incomes propped up the town's ailing economy and so the shops never suffered the deprivations of cash-starved prairie towns.

So widely known as a regional subculture did the Longstockings become that, even in 1955, curiosity spurred *Maclean's* magazine to send a Toronto writer to the area to investigate. The picture painted in "The Last Stronghold of the Longstockings," which suggests the sun had long ago set on the group, was not flattering. Many local readers dismissed the author's views as pure poppycock. Nevertheless, the impression clearly endured, as evidenced in one 1969 guidebook to Vancouver Island. Noted the author of the book (now out of print) in its description of the Cowichan area: "'Duncan?' says the average Canadian. 'That's where all the funny Englishmen live.'"

Indo-Asian Communities

Another large group that joined the Cowichan scene along with the first cast of European immigrants was made up of workers from China, Japan and India. Fledgling companies welcomed labourers from everywhere in the world to come and fill jobs in the island's fast-growing lumber camps, mines and road- and railway-building projects.

Most Cowichan communities had Chinese settlements. These were originally made up of men who had worked on railway construction or in mining and then moved on to other jobs, many opening up general stores, grocery shops and gambling joints. The main social centre for the Cowichan's Chinese community was Duncan. Today's provincial law courts stand on the site of Duncan's Chinatown. In 1969 the city ordered the old stores and apartments torn down and the families moved. At the last minute, some of the wood from the old buildings was salvaged and used to construct more than a dozen new structures—featuring wide porches and verandas, elaborate wood embellishments on the exterior and brightly painted finishes—at the Whippletree Junction shopping area on the highway south of Duncan.

Like the Chinese, Japanese immigrants arrived in the Cowichan early and worked in the area's sawmills, fishing industry and farms. Many later started successful commercial businesses. The first all-Japanese Boy Scout troop in Canada was started in Chemainus in 1929. During World War II, all BC citizens of Japanese descent were forcibly uprooted from their homes and moved to internment camps in the interior of the province. Those living in the Cowichan were no exception, despite many of them and their parents having been born in Canada, and despite how deeply and fully involved they were in their town or village. Their homes, businesses and other assets were expropriated or sold. When internment ended after the war, some families did return to the island even knowing they had to start over where they'd left off.

As happened everywhere across the province, many immigrant labourers led a marginal existence in this frontier land. A few, however, prospered impressively and helped others do the same. Two Indo-Canadians stand out.

Harbanse Singh "Herb" Doman, born in Duncan in 1932, was the son of Punjabi immigrants.

At the age of 12, when his father died, Doman left school to help support the family by selling firewood and sawdust door to door. By 33 he was the millionaire owner of Doman Industries, a building supplies retailer. He went on to construct sawmills in Ladysmith, Chemainus, Cowichan Bay and Nanaimo, cultivating a billion-dollar empire. Although the company eventually toppled in 2004, brought down by complications from swelling debt burden and declining commodity prices, the Doman name remains synonymous with the golden era of forestry in the Cowichan. He died in 2007.

The other key figure is Mayo Singh, who arrived on Vancouver Island via San Francisco and Vancouver. In 1916 the young Punjabi bought property and timber rights from the E&N Railway just south of the present-day highway to Cowichan Lake. In a decade he built up one of the region's largest inland logging and sawmill operations. Just as remarkable as his success was the community that flourished near the mill, an original global village of 1,500 East Indian, Chinese, Japanese and European forestry workers and their families.

The settlement started out being called Mayo, but postal confusion with Mayo, Yukon, forced a name change. Mayo Singh chose Paldi after his home village. In her 1997 book *Paldi Remembered,* Joan Mayo, daughter-in-law of Mayo Singh, describes a place where different cultures followed their own religious and social practices yet mixed daily in a tight-knit community overseen by the benevolent Mayo Singh. "Any cultural barriers that might have been felt elsewhere were crossed again and again each day. Children ran from house to house and Mayo Singh was looked to as a kindly grandfather." This was a place that welcomed a Japanese Buddhist temple as much as a Sikh temple, and where a kind of "Paldi English" evolved as the various resident cultural groups tossed snippets of their own language into the village's

Below: Paldi residents at a funeral pose before the temple, 1936. Mayo Singh built the first Sikh temple in Paldi in 1918. The community once had the largest Sikh congregation in Canada.
Cowichan Valley Museum 2007.2.2.71

Opposite bottom: Fong Yen Lew opened his Hong Hing store in Chemainus in 1915 and kept it going until the 1950s. This mural, often called the "Black Cat mural," was painted by Paul Marcano in 1982.

communal English-language pot. Even Paldi's annual Punjabi *Jor Malla*, a three-day religious festival combined with sporting events, drew support from the whole community. As Joan Mayo recalls in her book, "whole busloads of holidayers" from Sikh communities in Vancouver, Victoria and Lake Cowichan came for the festival. All the guests would be put up in Paldiites' homes and the mill's bunkhouses, and then everyone would participate in or watch the days of celebration and competitions that included wrestling, shot put, soccer, volleyball and running.

Newspaper articles about Mayo Singh's accomplishments described him variously as the "Cowichan Lumber King" and "one of the wealthiest men in the district." He always dressed in a three-piece suit with white shirt and tie and could often be seen in his Rolls-Royce fitted with railway wheels. The fancy car served two purposes: to take him out to inspect his company's logging operations and, in keeping with Workers' Compensation Board regulations, to serve as an emergency vehicle up the line when crews were working. It was Mayo Singh's lack of pretention and his unflagging generosity that made him just as memorable. Right up until his death in 1955, many Victoria and Cowichan hospitals benefited from his annual donations.

Today Paldi is a ghost of its former self, a small collection of homes and the Sikh temple, which is still active. The mill closed in 1945, the school and post office in 1969. Paldi became for a few years, as Joan Mayo puts it, "a haven for Hippies" who "took over every abandoned shack they could." By 1975 all the Japanese and Chinese families had moved away, and only a few East Indian families remained. Redevelopment of the old townsite has been proposed in recent years, but the likelihood of that prospect remains uncertain at this point.

Above: The Japanese temple in Paldi, between Duncan and Cowichan Lake, 1924.
Kaatza Station Museum and Archives P991.8.19

Growing Prosperity

Since the first settlers cut down trees to clear a patch for growing hay and potatoes, the Cowichan's two main resource economies have been agriculture and forestry. A benign climate and the fertile soils of the broad Cowichan and Chemainus river valleys favoured farmers. Dairy farming boomed even before 1900, and the Cowichan became renowned across the island for the quality of its milk and butter. The Cowichan Co-operative Creamery formed in 1896 to leverage dairy farmers' efforts further. The coming of the railway advanced the Cowichan's agricultural prosperity even more, giving egg, poultry, hog, sheep and beef farmers a means of getting their products to market. Cowichan asparagus, sweet pea seeds, honey and holly were on the list that built the region's reputation as a highly productive pocket of the West Coast.

One of the longest-running agricultural fairs in BC is the annual Cowichan Exhibition. It began in 1867 as the St. Peter's Church Harvest Dinner. From that modest origin it evolved into the Cowichan Fall Fair held in Maple Bay and then into the Cowichan Exhibition. The exhibition fairgrounds were long located in Duncan but after 2008 moved to a larger property in North Cowichan.

Logging and sawmilling reigned in virtually every corner of the region, abetted by the ever-expanding railway service that opened up the seemingly limitless wood supply in the Cowichan's famous forests. In the early days, logging was done entirely by hand, and the transport of the logs relied on ox- and horsepower. To tackle the big coastal trees, men stood on springboards, usually two metres (seven feet) or more above the ground, stuck into either side of the trunk. It could take a couple of handloggers armed with axes, crosscut saws, wedges and sledge hammers the better part of a day to drop a tree that was more than two metres (seven feet) in diameter. Once the tree was felled, it was bucked up into shorter, more manageable lengths. The timber was then dragged by oxen or horse team to a skid road (a rough track built

Top and left: The Cowichan Exhibition is the region's largest agricultural fair and one of the longest-running fairs in BC.

Above: The tractor-pull competition during the 140th Cowichan Exhibition.

Duncan, Chemainus, Ladysmith and Region

Above: About one-quarter
of Vancouver Island's
productive farmland lies in
the Cowichan region.

Opposite: Big farms require
big watering systems.

of half-buried logs laid side by side across the road) and skidded down to the water—an arduous and highly dangerous task, given the massive size of the pieces and their tendency to roll. Gradually, many logging companies built their own small rail lines to get their logs out of the woods first to sorting grounds and then on to tidewater. As roads into the Cowichan's interior improved, trucks eventually became a more efficient and versatile mode of log transport.

Less known is the Cowichan's past mining action. Lime was once quarried in vast quantities at both Bamberton and Cobble Hill. Gold, silver and manganese were also mined at several locations. The region's biggest mining story, however, is copper. The King Solomon mine by the upper Koksilah River and the Blue Grouse mine near Honeymoon Bay yielded ore, but it was Mount Sicker that briefly became one of the province's biggest copper-producing sites. The ore body discovered there in 1895 sparked such a bonanza of investment, activity and high hopes that by 1903 three separate mines tapped into the same haunch of Big Sicker Mountain. The frenzy that followed put the communities of Westholme, Chemainus, Ladysmith, Duncan and soon-to-be-built Crofton on the lips of industrialists, bankers and emigrant miners around the world.

The Lenora mine was owned by Henry Croft, a mining engineer, businessman and brother-in-law of James Dunsmuir, who was a major stakeholder in the competing Tyee mine. It was a feverish, international headline-grabbing time that fell apart in less than 10 years. The story of the mountain's meteoric rise and fizzle turns largely on the epic feud between its two main players, Croft and Dunsmuir. Estranged and bitter over family matters, they spent wildly in building parallel infrastructures to get their ore out of the ground, down the mountain and

The *Spirit Pole*, designed by First Nations artist, carver and singer Carey Newman, is a legacy of the 2008 North American Indigenous Games. The pole stands outside the Cowichan Aquatic Centre.

Natives and non-Natives join forces to sing and drum at the opening ceremonies of the North American Indigenous Games in Duncan in August 2008.

into the separate copper smelters they'd built, Croft in Crofton and Dunsmuir in Ladysmith. Falling copper prices didn't help, and in the end both enterprises failed. By 1908, Mount Sicker's mines were quiet and its houses and businesses empty.

Modern First Nations

Today in the region the registered aboriginal population numbers well over 7,200, of whom 20 percent are Métis. Cowichan Tribes, with nearly 5,000 members, is the largest First Nations group in the province. Each of the region's First Nations has its own government, run by an elected chief and council.

The last few decades have been a particularly high-profile time for Cowichan Tribes. The business-minded, progressive group now manages close to $60 million in revenues annually. Its business arm, Khowutzun Development Corporation, owns several companies, including Cherry Point Vineyards and the Quw'utsun' Cultural and Conference Centre. It's also one of the biggest employers in the region. The current chief of Cowichan Tribes is Lydia Hwitsum, elected in the fall of 2007. Chief Hwitsum, who has served two previous terms in this position, holds a law degree and a diploma in public sector management, has worked with the United Nations as an advocate for indigenous rights and sits on the University of Victoria's board of governors.

In August 2008 Cowichan Tribes hosted the biggest event ever held in the region's history, the North American Indigenous Games. The games, called NAIG for short, were first held in Edmonton, Alberta, in 1990 and have since been staged every two to three years in Canada or the US. During the Cowichan event, an estimated 20,000 people—including spectators, 5,000 athletes on 28 teams from across North America, and 3,000 artists, dancers and other performers—came together for a week of competition and cultural celebrations that attracted national attention. The sports that make up the games range from the indigenously traditional such as archery, canoe racing, lacrosse and wrestling to the non-traditional such as basketball, golf, tae kwon do and volleyball.

A lacrosse match under way at Fuller Lake Arena near Chemainus during the North American Indigenous Games. An estimated 5,000 athletes from 28 teams participated in the games.

The Cowichan

The Cowichan Sweater

The Cowichan sweater is perhaps the region's most quickly recognized product. In the face of much imitation, its local makers have defied mass-market, machine-generated look-alikes by continuing to make the unique garments. For decades, dignitaries have been presented with this quintessentially BC gift. Recipients range from royal family members to US presidents and Canadian prime ministers. Not only that, the Cowichan sweater has gained a hip following, a discerning international clientele of rock stars and the otherwise culturally attuned. What makes the Cowichan sweater so cool is its history ("textile technique fusion," as anthropologists put it), distinctiveness, genuine functionality and the fact that every single one is hand knitted to patterns that are, like treasured recipes, special to the knitter's family.

Well before European contact, the Coast Salish people generally were adept at weaving materials such as mountain goat hair and plant fibre. So when the Cowichan people were introduced to knitting by the Sisters of St. Ann at Tzouhalem, they picked up the technique quickly. Pioneer women helped to keep the craft going. One of these women, Jemima Colville, is credited with teaching her Cowichan neighbours the Fair Isle pattern to which they then added their own flair. The Cowichan sweater was born.

Only undyed sheep's wool is used in authentic Cowichan sweaters. The lanolin in the wool naturally repels water, making the garments durable and practical for damp climates. Another sign of an authentic Cowichan sweater is that it is made in one piece, with seams hand sewn afterward. For zipped sweaters, a modern adaptation, the zippers are sewn in by hand. All authentic sweaters are also marked by a registration number and the name of the knitter.

In 2007 public appeals were made to the Canadian Olympic Committee to adopt the Cowichan sweater as the official wardrobe item of Canadian athletes in the 2010 Winter Olympics and Paralympics in BC. The suggestion filled the

The distinctive Cowichan sweater is now recognized in many parts of the world.

news and even reached the floor of the province's legislative assembly. Duncan knitter Emily Sawyer-Smith created a special Olympic-rings-and-maple-leaf design, and two sweaters she made were presented to Premier Gordon Campbell and International Olympic Committee president Jacques Rogge. It disappointed many that the idea was not picked up, but no matter: the cachet of the Cowichan sweater around the world continues to keep these one-of-a-kind articles in demand.

Now Playing in the Cowichan

The Cowichan's economy has shifted greatly in recent years. The forest industry remains a major player, supporting a host of woods-based activities from road engineering and logging to value-added milling, pulp production and manufacturing of building products. And the largest forest company on the coast, Western Forest Products, is based in Duncan. That said, although the forest sector has historically been the region's revenue and employment backbone, the industry has lately been in steady decline. Even before the global economic recession struck in the fall of 2008, declining world demand for wood fibre and pulp had already added to local market woes caused by the long-running dispute between Canada and the US over the latter's tariff on this country's softwood lumber exports.

The train between Victoria and Courtenay makes scheduled stops at several Cowichan stations.

Fortunately major investments in commercial, retail, and housing and condo properties over the last decade have invigorated the region in a new way. Newcomers are discovering the Cowichan in record numbers, drawn by its setting, amenities, affordability and commutability to Nanaimo and Greater Victoria. In the light industry sector, businesses such as furniture and kayak manufacturing have set up shop. Agriculture, notably dairy farming, continues as a mainstay. The commercial fishing industry has largely disappeared; processing plants in the region have closed and wild fish stocks are in decline. Nevertheless, other parts of the marine sector—marine supplies and sales, recreational boating, sport fishing, fish hatcheries and aquaculture (fish farms, raising mainly salmon and shellfish)—have remained steady. The newer sectors of outdoor recreation and agri-tourism are thriving.

All of this has been welcome news for a region whose economic fortunes once relied so heavily on forestry. The hits suffered by the industry have hurt, but diversification is helping buffer the impact.

Since Canadian Pacific Railway sold the E&N in 1999, uncertainty has plagued the line's long-term prospects. Each time the axe has nearly dropped, public pressure has diverted the fatal blow. VIA Rail operates a Dayliner service now, and some freight use has been resurrected. Fuelled by the growth in the Cowichan's population, calls to turn the rail into a first-class commuter service are now possibly as persistent as the calls Sir John A. Macdonald heard at Duncan's Crossing in 1886 for a local E&N station. The significant costs to upgrade the line before any expanded service is feasible remain to be weighed against investments in other transport modes to serve the swelling over-the-Malahat population.

3

South Cowichan

For many people living on the southern tip of Vancouver Island, heading "over the Malahat" carries with it a dash of derring-do. In reality the stretch up and across Malahat Ridge from Goldstream Park to Mill Bay is only 25 kilometres (15 miles) long, mostly two-lane in both directions and one of the best maintained portions of the entire Trans-Canada Highway on the island. At its highest elevation, the Malahat Drive reaches 356 metres (1,168 feet) above sea level.

The journey so moved early 20th-century poet Bliss Carman that he wrote a five-verse tribute titled "Malahat." Only a cynic would choose to interpret "A paradise in blue and green / That make the amazed heart stand still" or "A glimpse of heaven from Malahat" as meaning Carman had anything but a scenic ride.

The road over the Malahat was built in 1910 and opened in 1911. It replaced the original rough wagon track, the Goldstream Trail, that went north from Victoria by first going west through the Sooke Lake area

Many homes in Cowichan Bay's "downtown" lie on or perch beside the water, giving residents front-door access to the area's boating playground.

"Go Slow Here," the sign advises motorists like these 1914 travellers on the first road built over the Malahat.
BC Archives E-00422

Below: The Aerie Resort and Spa has a view southeast, overlooking Finlayson Arm.
Courtesy of Aerie Resort and Spa

Opposite: The Malahat today is part of the Trans-Canada Highway.

and on to Shawnigan Lake and Cowichan Bay. While the new route was more direct and improved land travel between south-island and up-island communities, the narrow gravel road was not for nervous drivers or nervous passengers. At spots where the road ran right across the ridge's steep flank, the slope on the downhill side dropped precipitously toward Saanich Inlet. Falling rock from the uphill side of the road posed at best an inconvenience and at worst a danger to vehicles and their occupants. So did mud slides, which could bring rain-saturated soils cascading down from above the road or cause the lower outside edge of the road itself to disappear. The wise motorist tackled the Malahat Drive prepared with spare tires, a supply of water to cool an overheated radiator, a provision of food, water and blankets in case of a breakdown, and a prayer for fair weather and safe road conditions.

Over the years as the road was upgraded, the scenic merits of the Malahat Drive were increasingly promoted, as they still are. In 1956 the road was substantially widened, straightened along some sections and in other ways modernized. Being part of the Island Highway, now officially part of the Trans-Canada Highway, has helped keep the Malahat route in good shape and able to cope with the growth in traffic moving up and down the island.

Both this section of highway and the sparsely populated, unincorporated area here called Malahat are named for the Malahat First Nation. The ancestors of the Malahat people used the ridge's caves for spiritual purposes. Still today First Nations consider the Malahat to be one of the most sacred sites on the southern island.

Attractions in this area include the Aerie Resort and Spa (dripping in awards-bling from *Condé Nast Traveler, Travel & Leisure* and other magazines and organizations) and the considerably more modest Spectacle Lake Provincial Park, which is high enough to become a winter playground some years for skaters and cross-country skiers.

On the downhill run of the Malahat's north side, the turnoff for Bamberton Provincial Park descends to water's edge on Saanich Inlet. Next door to the park is the former Bamberton townsite. From 1905 to 1970 British Portland Cement Manufacturers quarried the limestone out of the hillside here and turned it into "grey gold." According to the Bamberton Historical Society (based in Mill Bay), at one time every major construction project in the province—roads, dams, airports, mines—and many around the world were built with Bamberton cement. The town of 150 emptied when the plant shut down and the quarry was abandoned.

In the years since, various developers have dreamed of resurrecting a community, much bigger than the original Bamberton, on the 688-hectare (1,700-acre) waterfront property. Public and environmental groups have trampled flat such notions, citing concerns over site capacity, water availability, environmental damage to the inlet and surging traffic volume on the highway. All proposals have been snuffed out, but the vision of a reborn Bamberton seems too attractive to be let go. The latest idea for the site proposes a mixed residential and commercial community of more than 8,000 "with sustainability as a key feature."

Mill Bay

Below right: A Mill Bay boating party c. 1900.
BC Archives I-58316

Below: The Brentwood Bay–Mill Bay ferry crossing has been promoted as "The Island's Most Beautiful Shortcut."

Mill Bay, overlooking Saanich Inlet to the Saanich Peninsula beyond, used to be a small, pretty and quiet community. It's still a pretty and quiet place but has grown like Topsy in the last 30 years, becoming a favoured bedroom community of Victoria. In the past decade alone its population nearly doubled to about 5,000. For all that Mill Bay is at its heart still a seaside village. Will this change if TimberWest Forest develops the 10,118 hectares (25,000 acres) it owns on the hills west of the highway? That's a debate being well chewed over in cafés and pubs throughout the South Cowichan.

Mill Bay's beginnings go back to the 1850s, when Henry Sheppard ran a sawmill near the bay. He soon sold out to W.P. Sayward, who expanded the mill into a major industry, and the name "Mill Bay" stuck. Were it not for the mill starting when it did, the place might have

been named Whalers' Bay. British Columbia's first commercial whaling business was set up here in 1866 by two Scots who contracted Hawaiians to hunt the whales and bring them in to Mill Bay for reduction. The operation dented the local whale population in three years, so the plant moved north to Cortes Island.

From here the Brentwood Bay–Mill Bay ferry provides a 25-minute trip across the Saanich Inlet, directly connecting the Cowichan region and the Saanich Peninsula. This route is said to be the oldest continuously operating saltwater ferry in the province. Brentwood Bay is next door to well-known Butchart Gardens.

Frances Kelsey Secondary School in Mill Bay is named for Dr. Frances Oldham Kelsey, who grew up in Cobble Hill and went to various Cowichan schools. During John F. Kennedy's presidency in the early 1960s, Kelsey was working as a pharmacologist for the US Food and Drug Administration. Even though under intense pressure from the pharmaceutical industry, she fought approval of thalidomide's sale in the US because of her concerns over its safety. Later proof that use of the drug by pregnant women resulted in severe birth defects earned Kelsey great respect for her stand. She continued working at the FDA until retiring in 2005 at the age of 90.

Brentwood College School started out in 1923 on the shores of Brentwood Bay, across the inlet from its present spot. It quickly became one the best-known boarding schools for boys on Canada's west coast. After fire destroyed nearly all of its buildings in 1947, the school relocated to the former Queen Alexandra Solarium site at Mill Bay, opening there in 1961. A decade later, it became the first all-boys boarding school in the country to start accepting girls.

Rowing at Brentwood is serious business. The school has sent rowers to 9 consecutive Summer Olympics, and for nearly 40 years it has staged an international rowing regatta each

Above and below: Brentwood College's international rowing regatta brings thousands of competitors and spectators to Mill Bay annually.

spring. This regatta has become the largest sporting event in the world hosted by a single high school. In 2009 more than 1,700 rowers from 36 rowing clubs took part in 50 different events. This is by far Mill Bay's biggest event and draws thousands of spectators.

Cobble Hill

Cobble Hill's deep agricultural roots remain much in evidence today. There is a Cobble Hill village centre, located west of the highway partway to Shawnigan Lake, but much of the area is made up of large and small dairy farms, nurseries, vineyards and orchards. Among the oldest established vineyards and wineries at this end of the Cowichan are Cherry Point, Divino, Glenterra and Venturi-Schulze. Here too is Merridale Ciderworks, the first estate cidery in Canada.

First settlers in this area arrived in the 1850s, spreading out from Cowichan Bay. Irishman James Dougan came here by way of Australia in 1868. Dougan (who could trace his ancestry to the 10th-century Irish king, Brian Boru) went on not only to carve a successful homestead into the wilds of "Bear Valley" but to leave a long legacy of Dougans in the area.

The E&N Railway's opening in 1886 really seeded the village. That same year Cobble Hill's post office was established. It's still going and is believed to be the second-longest-running post office in Canada with continuous service. In no time a well-appointed train station was

Children play at the Cobble Hill Fall Fair. The fair, held at the end of August, features livestock and fresh produce judging, equestrian events, blacksmithing demonstrations, arts and crafts displays and live music.

built, followed by the large Station Hotel, homes, shops and a bank. The first station master in town was Samuel Maclure who, after a short stint, handed in his cap and went off to study architecture. Maclure became one of the top residential architects in Victoria and across Vancouver Island.

By 1912 Cobble Hill was a full-fledged commercial centre and seen as enough of an up-and-coming place that the Victoria-based tent and awning company Jeune Brothers bought 121 hectares (300 acres) and created a 500-lot subdivision. The building of the new improved Island Highway in 1956 shifted the route away from the village, cutting the whole of the Cobble Hill area in half and siphoning traffic and shoppers away from the town. Many stores and businesses closed. Nevertheless, the village lives on with a pub, café, community hall and specialty stores.

How the name Cobble Hill originated is unclear. The underlying formations here are limestone. No cobble stones—by definition small rounded stones, larger than pebbles—are found here, though naturally deposited gravel hills occur in the area. One story is that the place is named for a Lieutenant Cobble of the Royal Navy. Another story is that an early English visitor said the area reminded her of a place called Cobble Hill in England.

The hill of Cobble Hill—called Cobble Hill Mountain—has a network of well-used hiking and walking trails. On its east side is Quarry Wilderness Park, a former limestone quarry that is now a local swimming hole.

Above: The Cobble Hill Farmers' Institute has hosted the community's fall fair since 1909.

Left: A young owner puts her miniature pony through its paces at the Cobble Hill Fall Fair.

Following pages: A frosty morning in late fall.

View over the south end of Shawnigan Lake.

Shawnigan Lake

Every August 13 Lori Treloar, curator of the Shawnigan Lake Museum, leads a group up to the E&N Railway tracks above the lake to wait for the train. The cairn at this spot, known as Cliff-side, commemorates Prime Minister John A. Macdonald's visit on that date in 1886 to pound in the line's last spike. As the train slows down, the engineer, passengers and Shawnigan group mark the anniversary with hoots, cheers and waves.

The E&N figures prominently in Shawnigan's historical development. It wasn't long after the twang of silver mallet striking golden spike had died away that hotels, guest houses and lakeside estates appeared and well-heeled visitors with them. What the Muskokas became to Toronto and the Laurentians to Montreal, Shawnigan Lake became to Victoria. By the early 1900s the community was a uniquely island cocktail of farmers, loggers and sawmill workers mixed with hotel proprietors, city "summer people" and nearly two dozen retired British army officers who settled with their families on the lake's west side.

Until 1907 trains ran on a schedule that allowed husbands to commute between the lake and Victoria daily. Excursion specials also brought holidaymakers by rail up to the lake, often delivering as many as 400 in a day (even 700 once), primed for days of water sports and

evenings of dining and dancing. The late historian and writer Bruce Hutchison, recalling his boyhood days at the lake in the early 1900s, was quite taken with what he remembered as Shawnigan's "elevated, dazzling and luxurious" social whirl. He wrote:

> *Every Saturday afternoon, before the Malahat Highway was built and the primitive automobiles appeared, a long E&N train brought crowds of weekenders, dressed in masculine white flannel and rustling feminine silk. They danced all night at the two hotels, recovered on Sunday and returned to Victoria, leaving behind welcome silence.*

The lake itself is about 7.5 kilometres (4.7 miles) long and averages about 1.5 kilometres (1 mile) in width. Participants in the annual Shawnigan Lake Walk cover about 22 kilometres (13.7 miles) walking or running. The hotels and summer-only cottages of the past have today given way to year-round homes, resort condominiums and other private holiday properties. Nevertheless, several public beaches and parks enable anybody to swim, fish or launch a boat. Waterskiing and ski competitions in particular have a long and glamorous history at Shawnigan. Yet as anyone who's been part of the lake for generations knows, a love-hate relationship with the motorized craft pervades the community. Summertime letters to the editor in local newspapers regularly rail against the activity and demand stepped-up noise bylaws.

Luckily many outdoor alternatives surround Shawnigan and those people seeking more peaceful pursuits can find them during the lake's craziest days of summer. Being in the Shawnigan area means having easy access to the Kinsol Trestle (see page 54) and the Trans Canada Trail. Renfrew Road, which runs along the north end of the lake, becomes gravel as it heads west, going all the way through to Port Renfrew on the Pacific coast, 65 kilometres (40 miles) away.

Shawnigan, like every other Cowichan community, has experienced accelerated development in the last couple of decades. Its population is now about 4,000. Much of this growth—like Mill Bay's—has been fuelled by increasingly easy access to and from Victoria and generally more affordable housing. Still many stretches of lakeside road and off-lake acreages retain a cottage-country feel. The presence here of three of the Cowichan's five private boarding schools also subtly exudes a reminder of the older, genteel Shawnigan. Even the heart of the village, now occupied by several attractive cafés, restaurants and shops, remains remarkably uncitified.

Top: The Strathcona Hotel, shown here about 1900, offered first-rate lakeside accommodation and handy train access. This and other hotels and guest houses helped establish Shawnigan Lake early on as an island holiday destination.
BC Archives C-03739

Above: The Shawnigan Lake Historical Society Museum occupies a former fire hall. What the museum lacks in space it more than makes up for in exhibit quality and informative value.

Summertime at Shawnigan Lake.

"People who come back to visit the lake after years away are amazed by how villagey 'downtown' Shawnigan has stayed," acknowledges Lori, the museum's curator since 2005. "There's still no traffic light in the centre of town, just the four-way stop like there's always been."

Residents like Lori and her husband Grant, with a lifetime connection to the area, have a greater perspective than others might have about the lake's changing face. Both retired to the lake from Victoria, settling on a property that has been in Grant's family for a century. "I know change is inevitable," says Lori, who spent childhood summers at the lake, "but those of us who have been coming here for so long worry mostly about how the extent of development might affect the health of the lake—its water quality, its shoreline stability, all that."

The Kinsol Trestle

Every community in the Cowichan has several individuals committed to researching and preserving the local history. Tom W. Paterson—TW to many in the Cowichan—is one of those. He has a broad knowledge of the whole region's past plus a knack for writing about events and tales in a way that brings them into vivid focus.

Tom cuts a striking figure. He's tall and angular, and in his trademark wide-brimmed black hat, he looks every bit the gentleman cowboy. Across the region people recognize him easily when he's out and about, mainly because of the photo that accompanies his weekly "Cowichan Chronicles" newspaper column. Fortunately he's affable as well, so that when he is recognized and approached, even by complete strangers, he seems happy to chat.

Applying his love of writing ("by grade four, I knew I'd become a writer") to his love of history ("it's in my DNA"), Tom has turned out thousands of newspaper columns and magazine articles and more than two dozen books, most of them since he turned to writing full-time nearly three decades ago. Born and raised in Victoria, the former *Daily Colonist* copy boy and then printer moved to the Cowichan in 1974. Tom now lives in Duncan.

"The story of nearly anybody I write about is always part of a bigger BC story, and in some cases, even of a world story," he's quick to say to anyone who might try to slot him as having a Cowichan-only focus. "Everyone in BC not of First Nations background came from somewhere else. The gold rush alone brought an enormous wave of settlers to the province, a big mixture of nationalities, religions and colours. Many moved on after their dreams of riches

The Kinsol Trestle
crosses the
Koksilah River
just north of
Shawnigan Lake.
It is the largest
remaining wooden
railway trestle
in the British
Commonwealth.

went bust and many went home. But as happened here in the Cowichan, thousands of others stayed and became the first to clear land, plant crops, open saloons."

Tom has also been a vocal and tireless advocate for preserving the Cowichan's heritage treasures. Sitting high on that list for a long time has been the Kinsol Trestle, which he and many others in the area fought for years to save, considering it to be as much a national and provincial historic landmark as a regional one.

The Kinsol Trestle, spanning the Koksilah River northwest of Shawnigan Lake, is no less than the largest remaining wooden railway trestle in the British Commonwealth. Originally named the Koksilah River Bridge, the structure later became known as the Kinsol, an abbreviation of King Solomon, the name of the nearby copper mine that closed in 1907. The trestle was built by the Canadian Northern Pacific Railway. Started in 1911 and finished only in 1921, the magnificent structure was used for nearly half a century for hauling forest freight. The trestle stands 38.1 metres (125 feet) high and curves at an elegant 7 degrees along its 187.6-metre (615-foot) length. When rail transportation declined on the island, however, the rail line was eventually shut down. The last train crossed the bridge in May 1979.

In 1986 ownership of the trestle and rail right-of-way transferred to the BC government, and the Kinsol became part of the Trans Canada Trail. After two arson fires worsened the structure's already deteriorating condition, the government declared the trestle off-limits to all users. For years it sat in a derelict state. Not only was it sad to look at, but the significant gap left in the trail forced users to make a long detour to get from one side of Koksilah River to the other. In 2006 the province declared the Kinsol too great a liability to leave standing

E.J. Hughes, Royal Academy of Arts (RCA)

The paintings of E.J. Hughes hang in collections around the world and command princely sums (*Fishboats, Rivers Inlet* sold for $920,000 at auction in 2004, for instance). Yet all who remember this 20-year resident of Shawnigan Lake and later Duncan recall him as a modest, soft-spoken man.

Edward John Hughes was born in North Vancouver in 1913 and grew up in Nanaimo. After high school he attended the Vancouver School of Applied Art and Design, where his instructors included Jock Macdonald and Frederick Varley. He spent World War II as an official war artist, and much of his work from that time is in the Canadian War Museum in Ottawa. Being discovered by Montreal art dealer Max Stern in 1951 gave Hughes the ticket to leave commercial art behind, make the Cowichan his home base and devote himself full-time to developing the distinct "stylized realism" that came to characterize his painting. In exchange for this freedom, Hughes gave Stern exclusive rights to all his output. Within a few years, Hughes's work hung in public collections across the country. The Stern-Hughes relationship lasted for more than 35 years.

Hughes was an accomplished printmaker and muralist, but is best known now for his paintings of coastal BC, many of which portray Cowichan scenes. In *E.J. Hughes* by Ian Thom, Hughes is quoted as saying, "I have painted in the Cowichan Valley for fifty years and it is the most beautiful place on earth."

Hughes received both the Order of Canada and the Order of British Columbia. Since his death in 2007, various plans to create a lasting tribute to the acclaimed painter have been initiated, including the casting of a bronze statue of the artist to stand in Duncan.

Artist E.J. Hughes, RCA, who painted the Cowichan landscape for 50 years, called the area the "most beautiful place on earth."

Photo by Lexi Bainas, courtesy of E.J. Hughes Gallery, Duncan, BC (www.ejhughes.ca)

and announced plans to dismantle it. This announcement provoked much public outcry and extensive debate about the relative merits of preserving or replacing the unusual span.

A particularly useful voice in the din came from a Shawnigan Lake company, Macdonald and Lawrence Timber Framing, which specializes in heritage wood restoration. Among its previous jobs were the Scott Terra Nova Hut and Shackleton Nimrod Hut in Antarctica and Stirling Castle in Scotland. When Macdonald and Lawrence concluded that restoring the Kinsol would be less costly than removing it and building a small replacement, even former naysayers were willing to reconsider. In what seemed the eleventh hour, the province reversed its decision to tear the trestle down. In 2008 approval for rehabilitating the trestle finally came through, with funds committed by various levels of government.

"The Kinsol is such an impressive bit of engineering," Tom says, "and it was a huge frontier undertaking. It's the kind of thing that people want to see as close to its original state as possible. They don't want to come here and find a replica or small replacement bridge with interpretive signs showing what used to be here. They want to see the real thing."

And now it seems they will. The commitment to restore the structure—for which supporters are now seeking national heritage site designation—means that hikers, cyclists and horseback riders will once again be crossing the Kinsol Trestle landmark on the Trans Canada Trail.

Shawnigan's Private School History

A beautiful lakeside setting goes some way to explaining why this small corner of Vancouver Island has been home to several private boarding schools in the last century.

Shawnigan Lake School, founded in 1916, is still running. Like Brentwood College, it has become known for its rowing program. The annual Head of the Lake Regatta hosted by the school is a season-opening competition. Lakeside Preparatory Academy, on 9 hectares (22 acres) of Shawnigan lakefront, offers a focus on English as a second language ESL programs, catering to international students who need ESL support. In the fall of 2009, the Dwight International School also opened, taking over the property that for the previous 20 years had been occupied by the Maxwell Baha'i International School (which closed in 2008). Strathcona Lodge School for Girls preceded both of these on this site, opening in 1927 in a lodge built by the Canadian Pacific Railway and later torn down and replaced. Strathcona Lodge School closed in 1977.

Shawnigan Lake School, founded in 1916.

The Cowichan

Entrance to the West Arm, Shawnigan Lake,
painted by E.J. Hughes, RCA, 1960.
Courtesy of the Hughes Estate and E.J. Hughes Gallery,
Duncan, BC (www.ejhughes.ca)

Cowichan Bay

As a body of water, Cowichan Bay is a bay's bay: it comes fully loaded. It's deep enough through the middle to accommodate ocean freighters loading wood products at the deep-sea dock. It's wide enough to give everyone who uses it—from freighters and other working boats to recreational sailors and paddlers—ample elbow room. It's protected enough to give boats and floathouses safe moorage even through the winter at the village's marinas and docks. It's shallow enough at the edges and estuary end to support intertidal eelgrass meadows and a bird paradise. And it's more than pretty enough to have attracted homes, restaurants, shops and lodgings along and overlooking its shores.

As a community, the heart of Cowichan Bay runs along a 0.5-kilometre (0.3-mile) stretch of road on the southwest side of the bay. Farms have long existed on the hills and fields above the main road, but the lower town perched just above tidewater has always been the commercial, industrial and social soul of the place. It's a colourful, tightly packed row of seaside cottages, shops, marinas, art galleries, maritime museum, restaurants and lodgings all looking out over a foreshore of hundreds of docked, moored or anchored boats.

Samuel Harris gave the Cowichan Bay hamlet its start. The enterprising Harris landed in the area in 1859, and about where today's pub patrons park, put up his first building. Four years later he got busy laying out a townsite for which he thought the name "Harrisville" had a nice ring. Next to his house he built the John Bull Inn, which served handily as tavern, grocery store and church. Although his wish for an eponymous dot on the map didn't stick, Harris would likely have the satisfaction of knowing, were he still striding the docks today, that his townsite on the bay is the one that's survived while several others on the estuary end didn't.

Giovanni Baptiste Ordano was another early settler who played an influential role in Cowichan Bay's development. A former bugle boy who witnessed several battles of the Crimean War, Ordano arrived at the bay in 1858, still only in his 20s. Genoa Bay, tucked in behind the north side of Cowichan Bay, is believed to be named for Ordano's home port in Italy. After Harris sold out to him, Ordano proved to be even more the entrepreneur than Harris and was soon running general stores, a hotel, a shipyard and a fishing business.

Top: A freighter loads up at the Western Forest Products terminal in Cowichan Bay.

Above: Sea dog.

Opposite: A great blue heron perches on old pilings in Cowichan Bay. One of Vancouver Island's largest heron rookeries—estimated at more than 70 nests—is located in a forested area near the bay.

Above: Active boat works and an art gallery share space in the old Cowichan Bay Shipyard building.

Right: The Masthead restaurant occupies what was once the Columbia Hotel, built about 1863.

The hotel he built around 1863, the Columbia, is the home of the Masthead restaurant today.

The Corfields were one of the first families to establish a farm on the diked estuary. They went on to build a general store and post office, and the community came to be known as Corfield's. Poet Robert W. Service, best remembered for "The Cremation of Sam McGee" and "The Shooting of Dan McGrew," worked for the Corfields for a few years starting in 1899. He submitted several poems to local newspapers, as well as finding time to compose ballads about the social life in the Cowichan, take part in local theatrical productions and fall in love. Service might have become known as the Bard of the Cowichan rather than of the Yukon had he not chosen to move northward in

1903. Another resident of the area who had a way with words was John Spears, renowned in the early 1900s for his mastery of Lilliputian writing. Spears gained an international reputation for such feats as writing 12,000 legible words on the back of a postcard (now held by the Smithsonian).

Tiny Corfield's was also the childhood home of Air Marshall Sir Philip Livingston, KBE, CB, AFC, FRCS, DPH, DOMS, KHS, ophthalmic surgeon, director of medical services for the Royal Air Force, and in 1948, honorary surgeon to King George VI. Livingston's father, Clermont, had moved the family to the Cowichan from the mainland when Livingston Sr. took over as general manager of the Tyee copper mine on Mount Sicker.

The Corfield name lives on as well in its connection to the South Cowichan Lawn Tennis Club situated on the estuary. This is the only tennis club in Canada that still has grass courts and it is widely believed to be the second-oldest lawn tennis club in the world after Wimbledon. The club was started nearby in 1887, "only 13 years after the modern game of tennis was

Top: Cowichan Bay Maritime Centre.

Above: Tennis is still played on grass courts at the South Cowichan Lawn Tennis Club, believed to be the second-oldest lawn tennis club in the world after Wimbledon. This Cowichan Flats tennis party took place about 1880.
BC Archives B-02357

devised," according to local historian and author David R. Williams, Queen's Counsel, "and only 10 years after lawn tennis was introduced to British Columbia by Chief Justice Sir Matthew Baillie Begbie in Victoria." The club was later relocated to its current site on land donated by G.T. Corfield. When Corfield died, his will stipulated that as long as the club maintained grass courts, it could stay on the property.

Today the club has seven grass and two hard-surface courts. It draws players from around the world to its annual Grass Court Classic tournament and the Vancouver Island Grass Court Championship.

The bay's maritime past is on display at the main street's Cowichan Bay Maritime Centre, a workshop, gallery and museum rolled into one. Skilled wooden-boat builders and volunteers—members of the Cowichan Wooden Boat Society—join know-how, labour and enthusiasm at the centre to build and restore small classic boats. Covered exhibit stations line the Maritime Centre's pier, and a pavilion at the end displays a private collection of model boats. A third part of the centre's water and wood continuum is Herb Rice's studio. A Coast Salish wood artist, Rice carves poles, doors and other functional and art pieces.

Downtown Cowichan Bay has enjoyed a big revival in the past decade. While forestry-related and shipping operations continue at the head of the bay, the only industry along the village's waterfront and docks is of the relatively light variety, such as boat-shed manufacturing and marine support services. There was a period when celebrities such as Bob Hope, Bing Crosby and John Wayne were frequent Cowichan Bay visitors, enticed by the fishing. The shine went off the place for a while later on, and by the 1990s, locals say, the seaside strip had started looking shabby. Then a couple of businesses decided that specialty food had the drawing power to bring area residents and highway travellers out of their way. It worked. True Grain Bread, Hilary's Cheese and Deli, and Udder Guy's Ice Cream are located on the main drag and helped kick-start a new upbeat era in the bay. In August 2009, Cowichan Bay became the first certified Cittàslow ("slow city") in North America, part of an international network that grew out of Italy's Slow Food movement.

At the same time, the village hasn't forgotten its salty roots and yearly hosts several water-based festivities. Some, like the Cowichan Bay Regatta and Cowichan Bay Boat Festival, have a long tradition. Others, like the Fast and Furious Boatbuilding Race started in 1985, are more recent inventions.

Cowichan Bay is North America's first Cittàslow ("slow town")—a community that celebrates and promotes living life in the slow lane.

Cowichan Bay's village charm.

Opposite: Sunset over Cowichan Bay, home to motor vessels, sailboats and freighters.

4

Duncan and Vicinity

If ever a place deserved a Who Knew? Award, it's Duncan. The Trans-Canada Highway runs right through it, and a driver's first view of the town is an eyeful of strip malls, service stations, parking lots, fast-food outlets and car dealerships. As a result many people get the impression that this *is* Duncan and feel they've seen it a hundred times elsewhere. What's to stop for unless you need gas, coffee or a restroom?

Only a few blocks west lies Duncan's real downtown: a clean, compact mini-city with a mix of century-old and new buildings arranged around small, tidy city blocks. People arriving here for the first time from the highway, whether by error or impulse, often react as though they've just stumbled into the Lost City of Ubar. Compared with the strip's cultural ubiquity, this mature, well-tended and humming town centre—a near-perfect example of the small-is-beautiful principle at work—consistently takes newcomers by pleasant surprise.

No one is more aware of the strip's bad optics than

Duncan hosts many festivals throughout the year, including the Christmas Festival.

local residents. A March 2008 editorial in the local *News Leader Pictorial* says, "As much as we know it to be false, it is difficult to ignore the fact most people outside Cowichan define our community by Duncan's ugly strip. . . . The economy is booming. Investors are looking hard at the Duncan area despite the strip's flaws . . . All this development should be powering more improvement of Duncan's strip."

The matter continues to be discussed and ideas considered for ways to beautify the strip and not interfere with traffic flow, but the problem is an undeniably complicated one. The growing investment, diversification and prosperity in the Cowichan over recent years will no doubt keep the topic in play.

Duncan

The administrative and commercial hub for the Cowichan Valley Regional District's population of 80,000 is Duncan, with a population of about 5,000. In 1912 it broke from the municipality of North Cowichan to gain independent cityhood, all 2 square kilometres (0.8 square miles) of it. More than a few newcomers to town are taken aback to learn that areas they think are part of Duncan really sit either on Cowichan Tribes' land or in North Cowichan, for example, the Cowichan District Hospital, the Cowichan Theatre, the Cowichan Aquatic Centre, the Cowichan Valley Arena, the casino and the Cowichan Commons mall. Happily the city's relationship with its larger neighbours is good, and much co-operation and cost-sharing of civic facilities avoids most sandbox yours-and-mine concerns. Still the reality is that outsiders and locals alike refer to pretty well everything in near-orbit around Duncan as being Duncan's.

The puzzling municipal boundaries aside, the situation for residents in this local jurisdic-

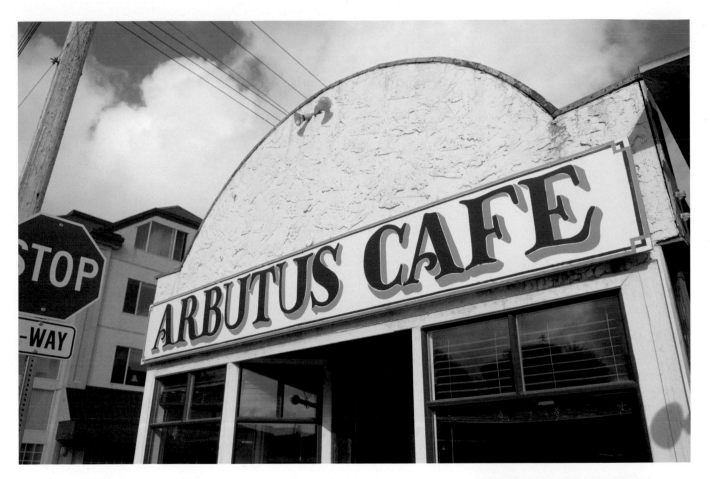

tional mélange is mutually advantageous on all fronts. Here's a place with virtually every service and facility you'd expect to find in a much bigger urban area, including a large well-equipped hospital, provincial law courts, a 731-seat performing arts theatre, a 1,400-seat ice arena and a full bells-and-whistles aquatic facility. For a relatively small place, too, there's a surprising concentration and wide range of public and private schools. One of these is Queen Margaret's School, built in 1921, the first private boarding school for girls on Vancouver Island. In addition to its strong academic curriculum, Queen Margaret's is well known for its equestrian program. The school hosts one of the premier hunter-jumper competitions on the island every May.

Duncan's downtown core is inviting, interesting and walkable. The streets are lined with attractive storefronts. Parking is plentiful and free. Cafés and restaurants abound. City Square is a public space that the public actually uses. And the E&N rolls into the centre of town twice a day, northbound and southbound, stopping at the old train station. The station, built in 1912, has received both city heritage status and federal heritage status (under the National Heritage Railway Station Protection Act). Since 2003, it has done double duty as a waiting room for VIA Rail passengers and as the Cowichan Valley Museum and Archives. The museum has assembled both permanent and special exhibits portraying the region's past, and offers summer walking tours of the downtown's historic points of interest as well as of the totems for which the city has become known. Parked beside the museum is one of only a few restored cabooses in Canada, brought back to 1940s splendour in the summer of 2008. The Canadian National (CN) caboose is hard to miss, painted as it is in Montmorency Orange, determined by the restoration team to be the right choice in keeping with the car's postwar-era origins.

Down-home friendliness and relaxed sophistication thrive in equal measure throughout Duncan's city centre.

Cedar Man Holding Talking Stick, carved by Richard Hunt, is the world's largest-diameter totem pole. It stands beside the provincial law courts in downtown Duncan.

Duncan, City of Totems

Duncan's outdoor collection of 80 totem poles adds a distinctive flourish of visual and cultural significance to the city's downtown. In the 1980s city council hatched the idea of commissioning Northwest Coast Native carvers to create totem poles for display along the city's streets and in its parks. The idea was both to showcase First Nations artistry and craftsmanship and to draw visitors to Duncan to view the open-air display of colourful, imagery-laden poles.

Among the first carvers to be approached were three from the Cowichan region, Tom and Doug LaFortune and Francis Horne. As interest in the project grew, artists and carvers from other areas were invited to create poles for the collection as well. A Maori pole is also part of the collection, carved by Tupari Te Whata, who came from Duncan's sister city, Kaikohe, New Zealand, to join the Cowichan carvers. The newest addition to the collection is the *Spirit Pole*, designed by Coast Salish and Kwagiulth artist Carey Newman. The pole was toured through 45 communities in the province in the summer of 2008, returning to Duncan in time for the arrival of the crowds of thousands who attended that year's Tribal Journeys Canoe Voyage and North American Indigenous Games hosted by Cowichan Tribes.

One pole of particular note is *Cedar Man Holding Talking Stick*. It is the world's largest-diameter totem pole, measuring almost two metres (nearly seven feet) across at the base. This pole was made by renowned carver and artist Richard Hunt from a cedar tree estimated to have been 775 years old when it was found for this project near Port Renfrew on Vancouver Island's west coast. The pole was officially raised and dedicated in 1988.

Master carver Simon Charlie of Duncan was an internationally acclaimed Coast Salish artist who influenced a generation of young carvers, many through his studio in Koksilah. By his own reckoning, he carved the equivalent of 22 log-

Master carver Simon Charlie beside one of his totem poles in Koksilah, 1954. *Cowichan Valley Museum 2003.8.2.793*

ging truckloads of cedar logs into totem poles during his lifetime. His work stands in the Parliament Buildings in Ottawa, the Royal BC Museum in Victoria and collections all over the world. For his artistry and contributions to arts and culture, the Cowichan Tribes elder received the Order of British Columbia in 2001 and the Order of Canada in 2003. He passed away in 2005 at the age of 87.

While the big-box retail store giants have been investing in and around Duncan in recent years, the more than 100 non-chain, non-franchise businesses in the town draw many shoppers: the galleries, bookshops, clothing stores, shoe stores, stationery and gift shops, toy stores, home furnishing and decorating stores, antique and second-hand shops, cafés, restaurants, salons and day spas. Numerous free festivals and other events sponsored by the city or business associations also bring people into the core year-round, including the week-long Duncan-Cowichan Summer Festival, the Christmas Festival and the Duncan Farmer's Market, the largest such market in the region, started in 1914.

Then there's the Rain Festival. It isn't a large affair or one of Duncan's many official festivals. Rather it's a pick-up-game kind of event born of the ever-creative and leather-banded head of local music impresario and arts scene promoter Longevity John Falkner. Every February since 2002, Longevity has led a small parade of enthusiasts through the downtown, the Gum

The Cowichan

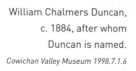

William Chalmers Duncan, c. 1884, after whom Duncan is named.
Cowichan Valley Museum 1998.7.1.6

Right: Duncan's heritage train station, built in 1912, today houses the Cowichan Valley Museum and Archives.

Opposite: View over Duncan, looking northeast to Somenos Lake, with Stuart Channel and the snow-capped Coast Mountains in the distance.

Bootin', Nose Flutin' Non-Precision Marching Band. Kitted out in colourful rain gear, the all-ages assembly plays an array of musical instruments, taking its cue from the first notes Longevity plays on his silver nose flute. In the words of the nearly two-metre (six-and-a-half-foot) tall parade marshal and music-meister, the event is "Vancouver Island's answer to a winter carnival—the perfect cure for the February blahs." For all its minor register on the region's calendar of seasonal events, the Rain Festival, just like its originator, reflects the warm, outgoing and sweetly quixotic nature of this town-like city.

As the Cowichan's long-enduring centre, Duncan has enjoyed the benefits of many resource booms and industrial enterprises. It could well have stayed just a quiet inland farming area had the route of Robert Dunsmuir's new E&N rail line not presented itself so enticingly near the property of early farmer William Duncan, and had William Duncan not had the pluck to envision a townsite named Alderlea sprouting up next to the rail line. The promise of a train stop that he and a local crowd managed to extract from Dunsmuir and Sir John A. Macdonald on August 13, 1886, made the town a reality. Alderlea never took, but Duncan's Station did, soon to be Duncan's and finally Duncan.

Thanks to the train, the area's agricultural and forestry economies burgeoned, and so did Duncan's fortunes. In the early days of the Cowichan's development, some of the best hotels north of Victoria were located here. The influx of moneyed British immigrants at the turn of the last century—the Longstocking era—also added an indelible embellishment to the town's

Duncan's Big Stick

Duncan has claimed since 1987 to have the world's largest ice hockey stick (and puck), but in truth it didn't get the official title for 20 years. In June 2008 the *Guinness Book of World Records* finally ruled that Duncan's—not Eveleth, Minnesota's—is the biggest.

The Big Stick, commissioned by the Canadian government for Expo 86, was built of Douglas fir reinforced with steel in Penticton in 1985 and moved to Duncan in 1987. It is 62.5 metres (205 feet) long and weighs just over 33 tonnes (about 36 tons). The stick and puck are 40 times the standard size.

The World's Largest Hockey Stick adorns the Cowichan Community Centre.

reputation, not to mention bolstering local coffers. As Tom Henry writes in *Small City in a Big Valley: The Story of Duncan,* "It was for the Longstockings' benefit that the shelves of Duncan's stores were stocked with English pipe tobacco, Eccles cake and the uniquely British concoction of lard and raisins called 'spotted dick'; that Mann's drugstore called itself a chemist shop; that Westwell's stocked copies of *Field & Stream, Tatler* and *Sketch*; that the Tzouhalem Hotel served a curiously unCanadian breakfast: kippers and grilled kidney on toast."

A construction boom in the town starting in 1912 produced several distinctive buildings, among them a new train station to replace the first one built in 1887; a new post office, suavely Italianate in architectural style (it became City Hall in 1975); the three-storey Cowichan Merchants' department store; and a new public school, a baronial structure inspired by the Georgian revival and designed by an acclaimed architect of the time, William Tuff Whiteway.

Another landmark, the Duncan Garage, was built a year later by Norman Corfield, who was credited with having been in the first team of drivers over the newly opened Malahat Drive, during which he clearly saw the way of the future. After 65 years the garage closed. Restored and converted, it reopened in 2003 as a multi-use commercial space and earned heritage building status. It now houses a mix of small businesses. One of those is the Duncan Garage Showroom, a cozy 80-seat performance venue that for more than 300 days of the year

hosts an ambitious range of live jazz, blues, folk and alternative music. The man behind the idea is Longevity John, the Rain Festival organizer. Longevity arrived in Duncan in 1988 from Ontario, bringing along a history of connection to Canadian musicians. (Back then he was Long John, but to avoid mix-ups with Brit-turned-Canadian blues legend Long John Baldry, he nobly volunteered to change his name.)

Partly through Longevity's connections and now partly through the music scene grape-vine, the Showroom has fast become a favoured spot for musicians, big-name and small, keen to perform in the intimate space with the great sound system. Among the Showroom's past headliners have been Bill Bourne, Phil Dwyer, Fred Eaglesmith, Stephen Fearing, David Francey, Amos Garrett, Garnet Rogers, Anne Schaefer and the late Willie P. Bennett.

Above left: A weekend festival in Duncan's City Square.

Top right: Longevity John Falkner.

Above: The "repurposed" Duncan Garage is home to a bookstore, organic market and café, and the Duncan Garage Showroom.

Somenos Lake Area

Located on the flats between the Trans-Canada Highway and Somenos Lake is the Somenos Marsh Conservation Area, part of a habitat network that includes the Cowichan and Chemainus river estuaries. More than 215 species of bird have been spotted in this 26.7-hectare (66-acre) property. The marsh received provincial protected area status in 1994 and later international recognition as a "globally significant Important Bird Area." Great strides have been made by public and private groups in rehabilitating the conservation area over the past two decades. From an elevated walkway and viewing platforms, visitors can take it all in and maybe even be rewarded with sightings of the rare Eurasian widgeon, great egret, tundra swan and red-throated loon. Also located nearby is a stand of deep soil Garry oaks, the rarest variety in BC, including what is believed to be the second-largest Garry oak in the province.

Top: Trumpeter swans in flight over Somenos Lake.

Above: Old forestry camp bunkhouses on display at the BC Forest Discovery Centre.

Opposite: No. 25, a 1910 Vulcan steam locomotive originally used on the Cowichan Valley Railway, tours passengers around the extensive grounds at the BC Forest Discovery Centre. The centre has a dozen historic locomotives.

Adjacent to Somenos Lake, the BC Forest Discovery Centre is an indoor and outdoor complex of interpretive and museum displays showcasing the island's forest identity. Trails and operating steam trains loop around the 40-hectare (100-acre) property through forest, along Somenos Lake and past an 1880s logging camp, a fire lookout tower and much early logging machinery. Among the indoor exhibits is a massive amber-coloured disc, the cross-section of a 1,300-year-old Douglas fir whose rings are annotated with the dates of key world events.

The man behind the centre was Gerald Wellburn. The long-time forest worker and ultimately forestry executive collected abandoned train locomotives, old donkey engines and other forestry-related machines and tools from the past. When his own backyard had filled up, complete with small railway, he began looking for a location to display the equipment and machines publicly. The BC Forest Museum was established in 1965. Wellburn remained its greatest booster over the years, leading tours and attending personally to visitors such as

Above: The blacksmith shop once located at Caycuse, Cowichan Lake, is now a display at the BC Forest Discovery Centre.

Far right: Children ride No. 27, a 1940 "Handy Andy" crew speeder originally used on the Cowichan Valley Railway.

Right: Tree rings at the BC Forest Discovery Centre.

Walt Disney. The story goes that it was on Wellburn's advice that Disney borrowed the idea of installing a live steam train at his little attraction in California.

Wellburn's love of British Columbia history and forestry were slightly outshone by his love of philately, a hobby he'd started as a boy in England. Acknowledged in stamp-collecting circles as having one of the best collections in Canada, Wellburn received five awards for his international collection. He also wrote the 1988 book *The Stamps and Postal History of Vancouver Island and British Columbia,* about which his friend Frederick Eaton Jr. of Canada's largest stamp auction house at the time (and a member of the former department-store family) says, "Here we are off in the sticks at the edge of the world, and we have international collectors buying copies of the book at $195 a pop. That tells you something about the quality of Wellburn's collection."

Cowichan Station

The small rural community of Cowichan Station has a "once upon a time . . . " feel about it. More than a century ago, its village centre sat near today's junction of Koksilah Road and Bench Road, adjacent to the E&N rail line. The concentration of homes there today—snugged up together along the narrow, winding road—hints at this past hub. Just down the hill, the combination of the narrow underpass beneath the short train bridge, the beautifully compact and proportioned St. Andrew's Anglican Church and the one-lane bridge over Koksilah River is enough to induce a time-travel moment in even the most no-nonsense passerby. Down a short side road is a modest wooden structure by the railway tracks where, with sufficient notice, the E&N engineer will stop to drop off or pick up passengers en route up or down the island.

Hard to imagine now, but in the 1890s Cowichan Station was the site of a large railway siding for the shipment of logs, lumber and farm produce. Around this grew up shops and businesses, two hotels, a community hall, a school and a post office. A fire in 1911 wiped out much of the village.

Although no longer a centre of trade and commerce, "downtown" Cowichan Station remains the de facto heart of the surrounding area that is made up largely of sprawling agricultural operations and small hobby farms. Blue Grouse, one of the island's oldest wineries, is located here, as is historic Fairburn Farm, which is the home of Canada's first water buffalo herd and a culinary bed and breakfast retreat.

Nearby Bright Angel Provincial Park straddles the Koksilah River and is a favourite spot for swimming. The park features a suspension bridge over the river as well as trails, picnic shelters and playgrounds. The land was donated in 1958 by long-time Cowichan Station residents Jack and Mabel Fleetwood.

St. Andrew's Anglican Church in Cowichan Station was built in 1906. Buried in its surrounding cemetery are many of the area's early settlers.

Koksilah River flows through Bright Angel Provincial Park in Cowichan Station.

Glenora

In the hills behind Duncan, bordered on the north by the Cowichan River, are the old logging and farming areas of Glenora and Deerholme. Many of the original homesteads in this area are gone now, but others have held on in whole or in part, abetted by burgeoning interest in small organic farm operations and the establishment of three wineries: Zanatta, Godfrey-Brownell and Echo Valley.

Vigneti Zanatta was Vancouver Island's first commercial vineyard. It was established by Dennis Dionisio Zanatta, who immigrated to Canada from Treviso, Italy, in 1950. He moved his family to an old dairy farm in Glenora in 1959. On the side he began experimenting with grape plantings down his fields' sun-soaked slopes. In the 1980s Zanatta's property became the site of more earnest grape-growing trials supported by the provincial agriculture ministry, assessing dozens of varietals to see which might show the best yields in the area's soil and climate. The Duncan Project continued for seven years before funding was pulled. Tentative results at that point suggested Ortega, Auxerrois and Pinot Gris might offer the best bets, but the report authors said that more definitive conclusions would have required at least another two decades of trials. Such testing has since been left to grape growers themselves over the past decade and a half.

Since opening in 1992, Vigneti Zanatta has continued to expand its vineyards and now has 12 hectares (30 acres) planted in more than 40 different varieties of grapes. Dennis Zanatta, often referred to as the godfather of the Cowichan's wine business, died in June 2008. His daughter Loretta, who trained as a winemaker in Italy, has managed the business and restaurant for many years with her husband Jim Moody, also a winemaker. Summertime lunch on the veranda of the property's 1903 farmhouse, overlooking the warm hills of Glenora, can be life-altering.

Barely a popped-cork distance down the road from Zanatta, a little deeper into Glenora, is Godfrey-Brownell Vineyards started by Dave and Ellen Godfrey. They bought the former farm property in 1998 and put their first vines in the following year. Dave was born in

Pinot Noir grapes destined for the wine vat.

Opposite: Guarding the grapes at Godfrey-Brownell Vineyards in Glenora.

Manitoba and spent much of his pre-Cowichan life in Toronto and Victoria, where it would seem he hardly had time to drink wine, let alone think of making it. A former university English professor, Governor General's Award winner and book publisher (one of his companies was the first to publish Michael Ondaatje), he and Ellen also once set up a software company that developed an early internet service provider. When all that was out of the way and his mind did turn to grape growing, Dave looked to the Cowichan and zeroed in on this Glenora land. By complete coincidence he discovered that he'd honed in on the 1886 homestead of a long-ago relative, Amos Aaron Brownell. It only seemed right to make Amos a posthumous partner in the vineyard and hence Brownell was added to the name.

Dave is grateful for the advice and guidance he got from neighbour Dennis Zanatta through Godfrey-Brownell's early years. The winemaking community, he notes, is largely a collection of independent-minded individuals. "Once I was putting together an anthology of the work of thirteen poets. Each of them wanted to get 10 percent of the book," he recounts and then, after a pause continues, "Winemakers are like poets."

Up in the northwest corner of Glenora lies the perfect nexus of former logging roads, abandoned railway beds and historic riverside fishing trails to yield enough route and recreational variety to satisfy any outdoors-lover. Access to the Trans Canada Trail here means a person could walk, cycle or horseback ride about 30 kilometres (18.5 miles) west to Cowichan Lake or about 17 kilometres (10.5 miles) south to Shawnigan Lake. Also here is one end of the 20-kilometre (12.5-mile) Cowichan River Footpath, a trail built by the Cowichan Fish and Game Association nearly 50 years ago, primarily for anglers. The footpath now lies within Cowichan River Provincial Park, which was established in 1995. It has become one of the favourite parks on the island for those seeking a quintessential West Coast outdoor experience with great ease of access by vehicle, bicycle, horseback or foot.

Cowichan River Provincial Park

Pretty well all of Cowichan River Provincial Park's 1,414 hectares (3,493 acres) lie within half a kilometre (a third of a mile) of the river's sinuous channel. The park extends along both sides of the heritage-designated river, from Glenora to Lake Cowichan, a distance of about 30 kilometres (18.5 miles). The park not only protects important stretches of the river but provides a wealth of recreational opportunities. Along its corridor are riverside walking trails, swimming holes, whitewater kayak launching spots and enough fish pools and runs to keep flyfishers content for days. At the eastern end of the park is the historic Cowichan River Footpath. A rough trail carries on from Skutz Falls west to Cowichan Lake. The footpath follows the river from Glenora to Skutz Falls, a route that includes several impressive crossings, with trestles at Holt Creek, Marie Canyon and 66 Mile and a suspension bridge at Skutz Falls.

The Cowichan River is one of the most praised fly-fishing rivers in all of BC. People come here from across the island and around the world to cast for trout (steelhead, brown, cutthroat and rainbow) and wild salmon (chinook, coho and chum). The Cowichan's brown trout, introduced to the river in the late 1880s, remains an especially sought-after species. Concerns over dwindling chinook and coho salmon stocks in recent years have brought many parties together—from the federal government and Cowichan Tribes to sport-fishing organizations

Alpacas are a common farm animal throughout the eastern Cowichan region.

Opposite: Tubing down the Cowichan River is a favourite summer activity.

Jeremy Koreski

Above: The Cowichan River at sunrise.

Right: After returning to the river where they were hatched, salmon spawn and then die. Their remains provide an important source of nutrients for seagulls, eagles and other fish.

A whitewater kayaking competitor in the annual Cowichan S-Bend Slalom race.

and others—to figure out how to reverse the trend. Steps now being taken or considered include more closely monitoring the river's water quality, improving flow management via the weir at Cowichan Lake, furthering hatchery and research efforts, and setting catch limits.

Recreationists also flock to the park to hike, swim and launch inner tubes or kayaks. Tubing, which involves floating downriver while sitting in a large inflated tire inner tube, is extremely popular. There are many spots to put in along the river. Depending on time of year, the water's volume and speed of flow, and a person's adventure level, a downriver trip can take five hours or more. While some sections of the river are quiet drifts, others are highly hazardous—a fact that is sometimes forgotten or not realized by those drawn to a nice low-tech activity like tubing. Fortunately several private outfitters in the region offer guided tubing trips, thus giving a novice a safer introduction to the bliss of riding the Cowichan's current downstream on a hot summer day.

Whitewater kayakers come to play and practise in the river's runs and rapids, as well as to compete in the annual Cowichan S-Bend Slalom race in the late spring. Under the whitewater river rating system, the Cowichan is considered a Class II to III river when its flow is 85 cubic metres (3,000 cubic feet) per second, and a Class IV when flow levels are higher in November to May during the rainy season and period of spring run-off.

Numerous day-use picnic areas and overnight campsites along the river give visitors ample opportunity to commune with the river as actively or mellowly as they would like. Near Stoltz Pool, a grassy picnic and campground site overlooking the river, also stands the Burma Star Memorial Cairn. It commemorates the Allied World War II campaign in Southeast Asia as well as the part played by Duncan's Major Charles Hoey. Just 30 when he was killed in Burma (today's Myanmar), Hoey became one of only two Canadians to receive the Victoria Cross during this campaign.

Farther west along the river is the 66 Mile trestle, a former CN rail bridge that crosses narrow Marie Canyon in which, far below, the Cowichan careers past the steep rock face. Upriver a little farther, at Skutz Falls rapids, a fish ladder aids spawning salmon in their uphill swim in the fall.

5

The Cowichan Lake Area and Westward

Cowichan Lake is what many consider the heart of the Cowichan. Cut long and deep into the interior terrain of the region, it lies about 162 metres (530 feet) above sea level. Kaatza, as it was called by the Cowichan Lake First Nation, means "big lake," a simple yet accurate description of the second-largest freshwater body on Vancouver Island (after Kennedy Lake near Ucluelet).

A much larger glacial lake once filled this depression, created by ice sheets during their retreat 10,000 years ago. After most of the water drained away, what remained was still a substantial body of water, measuring 34 kilometres (21 miles) long, about 2 kilometres (1.2 miles) wide at its widest point and well over 100 metres (328 feet) deep in some spots. To put this in perspective, it would take more than 10 Shawnigan Lakes to occupy the same area as Cowichan Lake does.

As if the generously proportioned lake, with its little islands and countless bays and points, wasn't

Dawn breaks over Cowichan Lake. *Chris Cheadle*

Top: Holiday houseboat
tied ashore for the night on
Cowichan Lake.
Boomer Jerritt

Above: The tall white
cairn atop Mount Prevost
commemorates those from
the region who lost their
lives in World War I or II.

spectacular enough as a natural setting, the surrounding mountains—many rising to over 900 metres (295 feet) and covered in thick forest—ensure that no viewer could possibly be unmoved by the place.

More than 6,000 people live in the Cowichan Lake area, about half of them in the town of Lake Cowichan and the rest in or near the small communities of Youbou, Mesachie Lake and Honeymoon Bay. While many newcomers, largely retirees and young families, have moved up to the lake over the last decade, the vast number of residents are part of a deeply rooted and closely connected network of families who can trace their local ties back several generations to great-grandparents and even great-great-grandparents. In the early 1990s a group in Lake Cowichan proposed putting together a book to mark the 50th anniversary of the village's incorporation. The response was overwhelming, with nearly 400 families contributing personal accounts, along with recent and past photographs, describing their connection to the community and what the community meant to them. The collection was published in 1994, fittingly titled *Family Trees: The Growth of a Forest Community*.

The main route out to Cowichan Lake is Highway 18, which connects to the Trans-Canada Highway just north of Duncan. As it heads west, 18 passes along the base of 800-metre (2,625-foot) Mount Prevost. It's common from this vantage point to see paragliders and hang-gliders circling overhead, one of the mountain's twin peaks being a standard stepping-off point to launch into the updrafts. Thrill-seeking mountain bikers also launch from the upper reaches of Prevost, blasting down from the heights through the web of old logging roads and trails.

The white 12-metre (40-foot) tall memorial tower visible on the mountain commemorates those in the region who lost their lives in the World Wars. A gas beacon once topped the

Above: Swimming in the upper Cowichan River in the town of Lake Cowichan.

Left: Recent development on the shores of Cowichan Lake.

The Cowichan

tower, flashing a light eight times a minute that could be seen 24 kilometres (15 miles) away. Also visible on Prevost's south flank is Averill Creek Vineyard and Winery, where the tasting room and outdoor terrace afford full-bodied views out over the lower Cowichan valley.

The first road from Duncan to Lake Cowichan, completed in 1886, was by all accounts an axle-busting, tailbone-bruising ride. The first motor tourist to try it out by hired car was Archduke Ferdinand of Austria, the same man whose assassination would later be the spark that set off World War I. The archduke's driver on this foray into the wilds of Vancouver Island was Captain Roy Troup of Victoria, who sent his rented single-cylinder Cadillac by train up to Duncan and from there chauffeured the archduke to the lake. The rest of the fishing party followed in horse-drawn carriages for the muddy five-hour journey.

The road was gradually improved over the years, making access to Hillcrest, Sahtlam, Paldi and other nearby communities easier. While the new highway allows for a quicker drive than Old Cowichan Lake Road does, the latter provides several access points to splendid Cowichan River Provincial Park (see chapter 4).

A road also circles around the entire lake, most of it built primarily as logging roads. Driving the 75-kilometre (47-mile) circuit is worth every teeth-rattling section where the towns' paved surfaces give way to gravel. Easier on the teeth perhaps, but a test of endurance otherwise, is making the trip on foot, which hundreds of participants do annually in the 56-kilometre (35-mile)

Great Lake Walk and Ultramarathon that the lake communities host every September.

Kaatza was an early place of contact between the Cowichan people on the east coast of the island and the Ditidaht (formerly called Nitinat) people on the west coast. In 1857 J.D. Pemberton, Vancouver Island's surveyor general, led the first non-Native expedition into the area. From the huge cedar stumps that he saw at the west end of the lake, he deduced that the local people "once manufactured their largest canoes there."

Forestry gave birth to all the communities and towns that still ring the lake. In the early days the dense brush made travel by land around the lake so challenging that the lake itself became the highway. For the same reason, floating communities became the norm. When logging operations moved to follow the timber supply on the mountains and valleys up the lake, the floating homes went too.

Already by the late 19th century, logging operators at the lake strove to feed timber to coastal mills at Crofton, Cowichan Bay, Genoa Bay or farther away. Delivering it from lake to coast was slow and difficult over the rough roads. Early logging companies tried using the river like a conveyor belt to send thousands of logs from Cowichan Lake to tidewater in the bay. Invariably these log drives created huge jams that caused flooding, erosion and stream diversions. Men were posted up and down the river to free snagged logs, break up debris jams and do whatever else was required—such as using dynamite to blast a jam apart—to keep things moving. In more than one winter, heavy rains during the drive raised water levels so much that the river heaved logs onto the banks and into farmers' fields and broke up Native fish weirs downriver. Bridges in the Duncan area endured a battering by the missile-like logs and required expensive repair.

The arrival of the E&N rail line to the lake in 1912 made it easier to get logs to the mills for processing into lumber, and the gates into Cowichan Lake's forest bounty swung wide open. In the woods, mechanization had already started to arrive as well, increasing the efficiency of the harvest. Steam-driven "donkey engines," which used long cables to winch and drag logs to skid roads, gradually replaced ox- and horsepower. The new technology was fraught with challenges, for machine and operator, as John F.T. Saywell so clearly describes in his history of the lake, *Kaatza: The Chronicles of Cowichan Lake*:

Above left: BC's first steam-driven donkey engine (or steam donkey) was put to work in the woods near Chemainus at the turn of the last century.
BC Archives B-06977

Above: Forest Workers' Memorial Park in Lake Cowichan honours the area's loggers and other forestry workers killed on the job.

The Cowichan

The hauling of the blundering, lumbering log of huge size through the obstacles of the woods was an exciting adventure in itself. The sudden shivering shock when the log jammed behind a rock, the ominous tautening of the cable, the jarring, whirring throb when the engineer hauls in the cable with a run to jerk the fallen log over the hindrance all put a strain on the stoutest engine.

Another advance, called high-lining, which lifted and moved logs about using a system of cables and pulleys rigged to tall trees, replaced the need for skid roads. And then motorized chainsaws came along, proving to be far more effective at most big jobs than axes and hand-saws. The invention and adoption of bigger, tougher and more effective forestry tools and machines have never stopped. These days heavy equipment—feller-bunchers, grapple yarders, skidders, delimbers and other types—is used for nearly every aspect of forest harvesting. Furthermore, road building and helicopter logging have extended access into remote and difficult terrain in a way the early Cowichan loggers never would have imagined.

What early settlers in the Cowichan had discovered about the area's salmon and trout bounty was also soon being promoted farther afield by enterprising locals. By the late 1800s Cowichan Lake had become a sport-fishing mecca, reeling in well-to-do anglers from across North America and Europe. The first Riverside Inn was built in 1885, and about a mile away, the first Lakeside Hotel in 1893. Both became popular and accommodated all manner of nobility, tycoon and celebrity. The lake's reputation continued to grow for decades. Even Edward, Duke of Windsor (briefly King Edward VIII), paid several trips to the "Fly-Fishing Capital of Canada," casting his line along with everyone else for kokanee (landlocked salmon), rainbow trout, cutthroat trout, brown trout and Dolly Varden char.

At the same time a large number of new residents of independent means were drawn to the lake and inclined to settle for a spell. Worldly, well-educated and sometimes memorably eccentric, these included remittance men, retired army officers and men of mystery. Dr. Richard Stoker, for example, had a log house built for him and his wife on Marble Bay in 1889. Stoker had been a lieutenant colonel in the Indian Army before moving to the island to throw himself into cultivating rhododendrons (while his brother Bram in London threw himself into researching Transylvanian folklore and writing *Dracula*).

Cassie Beech ran a dance hall with her husband at Cowichan Lake. Here she rides a velocipede on the E&N tracks in 1913.
Kaatza Station Museum and Archives P988.26.3

Colonel Andrew Haggard arrived at the lake in 1905. Like Stoker, he had a brother who wrote: Sir H. Rider Haggard, the hugely celebrated author of more than 50 adventure novels, including *King Solomon's Mines*, published in 1885. Inspired (or riled) by Sir Rider's fame, Colonel Haggard set out to write his own tour de force. *Two Worlds,* which came out in 1911, was described by Saywell in his history of the lake as "dealing with the contrast between the pioneer life in the 'wilds' of Cowichan Lake and the 'gay' social whirl of Victoria." It was not well received, Saywell added, "particularly by residents of Cowichan Lake."

Another writer who took up residence in a lake floathouse for a few years was international journalist, world adventurer and fly fisherman extraordinaire Negley Farson. He came to Vancouver Island, drawn partly by having an aunt and uncle—the Stokers—at the lake and partly by the fishing riches he'd heard about. For someone whose past partying companions included F. Scott Fitzgerald and Ernest Hemingway—whom Farson could reputedly drink under the table—Cowichan Lake in the 1930s may have been a welcome breather from a life of excess. Farson fished and wrote while in the Cowichan, turning out articles and essays, as well as a novel, *The Story of a Lake,* published in 1939 by Harcourt, Brace. A review in *Time* magazine two weeks after the book's release had this to say:

> *Last fortnight Negley Farson did at last crack up—but only fictitiously, in a semi-autobiographical novel about a famous US newspaperman who ends up drinking himself to death in a backwoods cabin in British Columbia. An awkwardly constructed, Lost Generation novel, teeming with love affairs, ineffective cures for alcoholism, [and] neurotic athleticism, it will be read for its confessional thrills. But it will arouse little sympathy, despite the alibi that its drunken hero is an idealist 'still searching for the impossible in love, still clinging to many of his childhood ecstasies and still uncalloused . . .'*

In a different vein, perhaps, the psychiatrist and psychotherapist co-founders of Gestalt therapy, Fritz and Laura Perls, moved from California to Lake Cowichan in 1969 to start a Gestalt community. Though the training facility did not operate for long, the "Gestalt kibbutz" became well known in therapist circles.

In recent years Cowichan Lake's economy, as in all forestry-dependent areas on the island, has suffered a thousand non-cuts as a result of a deflating BC forest industry. Tumbling lumber prices, a strengthening Canadian dollar relative to the US dollar and a few other factors initiated the puncture. The decline in US housing construction starting in 2008, combined with the 15 percent US softwood lumber tariff tacked on to Canadian imports, added the squeeze. Where once the rumble and whine of five mills could be heard around the lake, all is now quiet with no mills left. Nevertheless, a broader-based economy than in the past means that area communities are holding up well. Numerous developments of residential and recreational properties reflect the growing awareness of the area as a beautiful and affordable place to live, with all the benefits that small-community living offers.

The bell that originally hung outside the cookhouse in the logging camp of Caycuse is now displayed outside the Kaatza Station Museum in the town of Lake Cowichan.

A 1927 Lima Shay steam locomotive sits beside the Kaatza Station Museum.

Town of Lake Cowichan

The "foot of the lake," where the Cowichan River begins its 35-kilometre (22-mile) run to the ocean, was incorporated as the village municipality of Lake Cowichan in 1944 and reincorporated as a town in 1996. The motto on its official coat of arms reads *Copia sub umbra montanum,* which means "Abundance in the shadow of mountains" and nicely sums up what the town of 3,100 has on its doorstep.

Lake and river water—especially water level—figures prominently in this area. In 1957 a weir was built to regulate the flow from lake to river during the high water of the late spring and early fall. Summertime releases help keep water flow in the river constant enough to support fish and other wildlife. The weir is operated by Catalyst Paper in Crofton, under the direction of the provincial environment ministry. The structure was built in two parts. On one side are the control gate and a fish ladder. On the other is a boat lock, the only one on Vancouver Island, which enables recreational boats to move between river and lake when water levels vary in May to September.

Talk has gone on for decades of raising the height of the weir to store a greater volume of water as demand on the supply has grown. Years of lower-than-normal precipitation, such as those experienced over the past decade, have added to fears of water shortages. Still the weir-change proposition remains highly contentious. Private and business property owners around the lake are concerned about how water inundation would affect their land and homes. Others, including First Nations, environmentalists, recreational boaters and anglers, and users of the system's water for domestic, agricultural and industrial purposes, are concerned about how potential water shortages could affect the entire river system. In 2007 a group representing the diverse interests in the matter developed the Cowichan Basin Water Management Plan, which included a recommendation to raise the weir by 30 centimetres (12 inches). That recommendation was a key part of the plan rejected by the directors of the Cowichan Valley Regional District. The discussion has not ended there, however, and continues to make headlines in local media.

In Saywell Park, adjacent to the weir, is the Kaatza Station Museum and Archives. The museum occupies the town's original 1912 railway station, which was moved to this site after rail operations shut down. While passenger service to the lake on the E&N lasted only until 1926, freight service continued until 1985. By then truck transport had replaced rail as the preferred method of shipping products in and out of town, and the line's Canadian Pacific Railway (CPR) owners put an end to the train service.

Lake Cowichan's cafés and restaurants make it a popular end point or turnaround for cyclists who have come up the Trans Canada Trail from Glenora and points farther south. The well-serviced, friendly town is also the main shopping centre for the hundreds of campers and other vacationers who come to the lake in the summer. Lake Days, one of Lake Cowichan's three spring festivals, has been an annual event since the early 1940s. Among the weekend's activities are a parade, dance and the crowning of the Lady of the Lake.

One person who gazed at the clear night skies over Lake Cowichan went on to become a Canadian pioneer in aerospace medicine. Dr. William Carpentier, who lived in Lake Cowichan as a child and young teen, was physician to the astronauts on the 1969 Apollo 11 mission that carried the first men to the moon. During the astronauts' post-mission world tour, Neil Armstrong gave Carpentier the title WFP or "World Famous Physician."

The Cowichan Lake climate that's so perfect for growing big trees is also perfect for

In Lake Cowichan's Central Park, a fountain honours local lad Dr. William Carpentier, physician to the astronauts on the Apollo 11 lunar mission.

Opposite: View of part of the town of Lake Cowichan showing Bald Mountain and the lake's North Arm to the upper right.

growing many flowering plants. Richard and Susan Stoker realized this when they moved to the lake in 1889 and began collecting and cultivating native and non-native plants on their Marble Bay property. The couple joined horticultural forces with George Buchanan and Jeanne Suzanne "Susie" Simpson, and the four created a garden and nursery that by the mid-1920s had put Cowichan Lake on the maps of plant growers and breeders around the world. The couples' specialty was rhododendrons. By the time Richard Stoker died in 1931, they had close to 4,000 of the plants grown from well over 100 species. The Simpsons later bought the Stoker estate and continued to expand the gardens.

Fast-forward to 1967. Wishing to protect the property in perpetuity, Susie Simpson donated the estate to the University of Victoria. After she died, a committee headed by well-known naturalist Roderick Haig-Brown came up with a plan for developing the estate for its new purpose. In her honour, the university opened its Jeanne S. Simpson Field Studies Resource Centre in 1976. The 10-hectare (25-acre) property now includes lab facilities, accommodation, a dock and 8 hectares (20 acres) of virgin forest. Much of the plant stock was also moved, at the request of the Simpson family, to the University of Victoria. This provided the beginnings of the university's Finnerty Gardens. Another chief source of stock for those gardens was the Cedric and Gertrude Meyers property in Honeymoon Bay.

In recent years the university has given the town of Lake Cowichan and the Memorial Rhododendron Park cuttings and root stock from the original Stoker-Simpson estate.

The North Shore: Youbou

Near Youbou on the north shore of Cowichan Lake.

About 16 kilometres (10 miles) from the town of Lake Cowichan along the lake's north shore is Youbou, population around 750. Say "yoo-boo" and you give yourself away as new to these parts. The name is correctly if not intuitively pronounced "yoo-bo" after two officers—C.C. Yount and G.D. Bouten—of the Empire Logging Company, which began the first sawmill here in 1914. Logging and sawmilling had begun on nearby Cottonwood Creek a few years earlier, and Cottonwood was the name the settlement went by. When the CN track was extended out this way in 1925, Empire's general manager and president (Yount and Bouten respectively) saw the dawning of a new era and immodestly coined a fresh place name, Youbou. Not all the locals cared for this relabelling, and some took to calling the place Hoodoo. Their objections made headlines in Duncan newspapers but to no avail.

While waiting for the CN to build its line to Cottonwood Creek, the company was based on floating camps. Forest workers and their families, single men and even company managers all lived on the water in floathouses. This continued into the 1930s for about three-quarters of Youbou's population even though a company-owned townsite was officially established ashore on September 1, 1929. Gradually people did relocate off the water, taking up residence in the new company-built houses.

Youbou's days as a major freshwater mill town finally ended when the operation's last owners, TimberWest, shut the place down for good early in 2001. On January 26 at 3:10 in the afternoon, workers gathered to watch as the final log was cut and so, too, their ties to a place that had employed some of them for close to 50 years. Since then the town has been in transition, easing from booming forestry town to boomer recreational and retirement destination. New lakeside home developments have gone in, taking advantage of Youbou's considerable

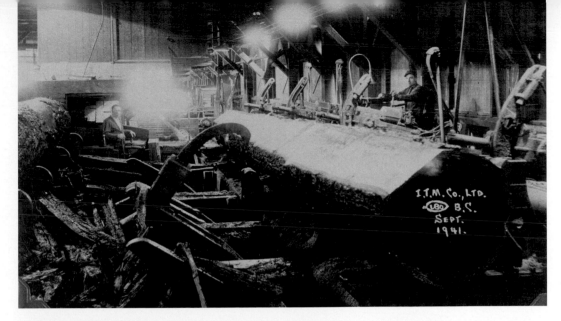

Part of the Youbou sawmill, 1941. *BC Archives E-02877*

Beach time at Youbou.

assets when it comes to offering magnificent water and mountain views. A larger project is also under way to develop the former 92-hectare (227-acre) Youbou mill property into a mixed-use site with a proposed 2,000 residential units, resort and small light-industry park. In this area, there is no shortage of parks and trails to suit everyone from level-ground walkers to experienced backcountry hikers. Many boating options exist as well.

Youbou's village core is small, concentrated along the main road through town, but the place has a close, neighbourhood feel to it. Many drivers heading out to campgrounds or cottages farther up the lake or beyond and into the Carmanah and Walbran areas do some stocking up here. Family events at the community hall are common, and every summer the residents host the day-long Youbou Regatta. Youbou also has the only sanctioned hand-set bowling alley in Canada. At Youbou Lanes, built in the 1950s with materials and labour donated by the mill owners, manual is a kind of business philosophy, not an operations weakness. Here, in addition to the pins being stood back up by human pin-setters, bowling scores are recorded manually and even the lanes are maintained by hand—dusted, stripped and oiled.

The South Shore: Mesachie Lake and Honeymoon Bay

Mesachie Lake

The South Shore Road heading out of the town of Lake Cowichan runs through the community of Mesachie Lake. The town of Mesachie Lake was born in 1942 when Hillcrest Lumber Company set up a sawmill here. The company not only neatly laid out a townsite and built its employees homes (many moved from Hillcrest's original base of operations in Sahtlam), it planted fruit trees along the boulevards to give a putting-down-roots look to the place. Since ending its time as a forestry-based village, Mesachie Lake has largely become a bedroom community for the town of Lake Cowichan. Still it maintains its own strong identity, holding events at the community hall and drawing crowds to the Mesachie Skydome for softball tournaments.

In international forestry circles, Mesachie Lake is known as the home of one of BC's forest research stations, established in 1929 by the BC Forest Service. The Cowichan Lake Research Station is recognized around the world for its experimental work in forest genetics and tree physiology, work that continues today and has made substantial contributions to the breeding and growing of commercially valuable tree species. In 1935, during the Great Depression, lack of funding put a halt to construction and research activities at the fledgling station. The situation was saved thanks to the Young Men's Forestry Training Plan, a provincial relief program for the unemployed. Under the program, 60 young workers moved to the Mesachie Lake property and got down to business building a cookhouse, bunkhouses, a water system and other facilities. A road was also constructed to connect the research station to the public road, thus eliminating the station's previous reliance on boats to ferry goods and people to and from the village of Lake Cowichan. During World War II, a work camp of Alternative Service Workers—conscientious objectors—was also set up at the station. The incarcerated men were pressed into tree planting and general labour, to the station's great benefit.

Honeymoon Bay

With a name like this, you'd expect a place of lakeside motels that advertise suites with heart-shaped bathtubs. There's nothing as gauche here. The story of the name goes back to the late 1800s, when a young bachelor from England living by the bay got so lonely that he decided to return home to find a bride. The general feeling among the other settlers nearby was that the fellow would return to the lake in short order with a missus, and with that expectation in mind, one wag dubbed the place Honeymoon Bay. The young man never did come back, but the nickname stuck.

The first settler in this corner of the lake was Englishman Henry March, who arrived in 1887 and began clearing the dense forest to create a farm. The site of the old March farm is now March Meadows Golf and Country Club, opened in 1970. It's the course where Dawn Coe-Jones, three-time LPGA tour winner and Canadian Golf Hall of Fame member, got her start.

Logging had been active here since the 1890s, but Honeymoon Bay really hit the map in the 1940s when it became a company town. Most homes on the original townsite were built by Western Forest Industries, which took over from another operator in 1947. As well as enlarging the existing mill, WFI invested nearly a million dollars to create an instantly beautified

Pink fawn lilies carpet much of Honeymoon Bay's Wildflower Ecological Reserve every spring.

Opposite: Wakeboarding on Cowichan Lake.
Boomer Jerritt

town, including directing that the 70 houses be painted different colours, an attention to detail unusual to see in company management at the time.

The mill has been gone for nearly three decades, and its Central Beach area now supports recreational rather than industrial use. Today Honeymoon Bay is a mixed community of young families, retirees, vacation cottagers and resort owners. It's also the closest town for supplies for vacationers at the large Gordon Bay Provincial Park campground. A legacy of WFI's operation here is the Honeymoon Bay Wildflower Ecological Reserve, a 6-hectare (15-acre) forest reserve said to have the province's largest known concentration of pink fawn lilies in springtime.

Farther west near the end of the lake is Caycuse. A small group of year-round residents live here now, but for 70 years it was a large logging camp. In 1927 the Cowichan Logging Company contracted with Empire Logging in Youbou to set up an operation on the lake's south side. Almost overnight, a floating hamlet of family housing, bunkhouses, cookhouses, offices and a store took shape. With enough children on hand that first year, even a school was built ashore, followed a year later by a community hall.

West to the Pacific Coast

From the Cowichan Lake area, a network of secondary roadways—most originally logging roads and some still actively used for that purpose—provides access south and west to other parts of Vancouver Island. The western Cowichan region between the lake and the coast is the traditional territory of the Ditidaht First Nation.

From Mesachie Lake, travellers can pick up the Pacific Marine Circle route, which leads to Port Renfrew on the Pacific coast. Port Renfrew is one of the main stepping-off points for backpackers heading up the coast along the famous 75-kilometre (47-mile) West Coast Trail. As well, the community is next door to Juan de Fuca Provincial Park, which includes Botanical Beach and the Juan de Fuca Marine Trail that runs southward down the coast. The road between Cowichan Lake and Port Renfrew is mostly unpaved gravelled surface, winding through rugged backcountry for about 60 kilometres (37 miles). From Port Renfrew, the circle route continues to Sooke, Victoria and then back up-island to the Cowichan.

Maidenhair fern thrives in the moist, humus-rich soils of the Cowichan's rainforests.

It's a two- to four-day drive over 255 kilometres (158 miles).

Gravel logging roads from the west end of Cowichan Lake lead out to Nitinat Lake and Carmanah Walbran Provincial Park, and from there connect with Pacific Rim National Park, and slightly farther west, Bamfield on Barkley Sound. Nitinat River Provincial Park, a day-use park for hikers and kayakers, was established to protect Roosevelt elk's winter range and the riverbank habitat of summer steelhead. Nitinat Lake, a 23-kilometre-long (14-mile-long) tidal lake, is connected to the Pacific Ocean by Nitinat Narrows, also called The Gap. Kiteboarders and windsurfers from around the world head to Nitinat between April and September to take advantage of the lake's strong and consistent winds.

The forests of the western Cowichan region are home to some of the oldest and largest trees in the world, including Douglas fir, Pacific silver fir, western hemlock and western red cedar. The Carmanah and Walbran river valleys are also famous for their old-growth stands of

towering Sitka spruce. One of these trees, called the Carmanah Giant, reaches 95 metres (312 feet) above the ground—about as tall as a 28-storey building—and is believed to be the tallest Sitka spruce in the world. Beneath such giants, with the sunlight filtering softly down through shorter trees and shrubs whose branches are layered with moss, hanging lichen and even ferns, it is easy to understand why people often compare the feeling of being in these forests to that of being in a cathedral. Making up the forest floor are deep, compacted layers of decomposing plant life, creating a ground surface that is spongy underfoot. It is in this nutrient-rich base that new vegetation rapidly roots and grows, hastened along by the humid environment. Forest scientists estimate that this ecosystem's biomass (meaning the total weight of plants per given area) is close to twice that of a tropical forest.

The Carmanah and Walbran area gained international attention several decades ago when logging that threatened to remove large portions of the mostly old-growth forests incited vociferous public protest. Responding to the outcry, the provincial government agreed in 1990 to protect first the lower Carmanah valley and then, five years later, the Walbran and the upper Carmanah valleys.

The Cowichan region extends all the way to the Pacific Coast. A long section of the rugged West Coast Trail, a magnet for hikers from around the world, skirts this area.

Josh McCulloch

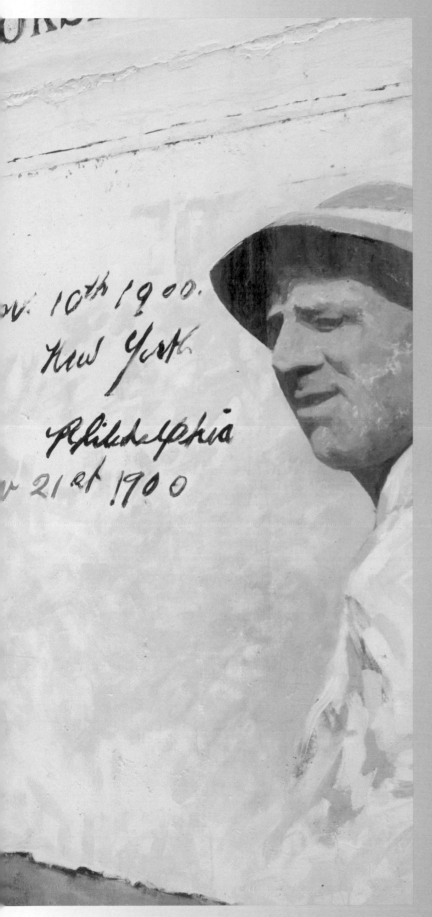

6

North Cowichan

Attending a music festival at Providence Farm, hiking on Mount Tzouhalem, kayaking in Maple Bay, lunching in Crofton, shopping in Chemainus, or even watching a performance at the Cowichan Theatre: a newcomer could be in the municipality of North Cowichan for days and not realize it.

North Cowichan—nearly 195 square kilometres (75 square miles) in area and with a population of 28,000—dwarfs Duncan, yet outsiders often miss its existence as a separate jurisdiction. It wraps around much of Duncan, reaches to the north end of Chemainus, extends west to the inland side of Mount Prevost and covers everything up the east coast within those bounds. It's mainly rural but includes several urban areas and small communities.

Incorporated in 1873, North Cowichan is the fourth-oldest municipality in BC. It once counted the young Duncan among its family of communities until Duncan opted for independence in 1912. The two households have always remained close allies, though discussion of boundary redrawing frequently comes up at the table.

Part of the mural *World in Motion*, painted by Alan Wylie in 1986, features the Horseshoe Bay Hotel and two of its most famous guests.

Above: The current St. Ann's Catholic Church and cemetery.

Above right: Long abandoned, the Stone (or Butter) Church still stands on the Cowichan estuary. It was completed as St. Ann's Roman Catholic Church, Comiaken, in 1870.

Around Tzouhalem

The road across the Cowichan estuary from the village of Cowichan Bay winds beside and over the meandering arms of the Koksilah and Cowichan Rivers, through Cowichan Tribes land, between farms and homes and past the road out to the mill and shipping terminal. A community called Tzouhalem was once here, a cluster of homes and a few businesses at the foot of the mountain of the same name. Within a short distance, four historic churches or church-affiliated buildings stand out: the Stone Church, St. Ann's Catholic Church, Providence Farm and the Anglican Church of St. Peter, Quamichan.

The noble St. Ann's Roman Catholic Church (better known as the Stone Church) on Comiaken Hill was completed in 1870. It was nicknamed the Butter Church because its builder, Father Peter Rondeault, made butter to trade for labour and materials. The church was abandoned only 10 years later when it proved too small to accommodate the growing congregation and its replacement, a new St. Ann's, was erected nearby. That church was heavily damaged by fire and later rebuilt. Today's St. Ann's Catholic Church stands in white splendour on a sunny hillside nearby, well maintained and steadily used. High above St. Ann's, atop one of Mount Tzouhalem's promontories, is a white cross. It was put there by Native and non-Native parishioners of St. Ann's in April 1976 as part of their Easter celebrations. The group carried the 91-kilogram (200-pound) structure up the trail that rises almost 500 metres (1,640 feet) from the church to this outlook. Climbing to the cross for an early morning Easter service has become a tradition for dozens of families every year.

Keeping a different kind of tradition, runners in the annual Mount Tzouhalem Gutbuster

The main building at Providence Farm.

follow race courses that go up, over and around mountain trails. Walkers, hikers and mountain bikers take to Mount Tzouhalem's trails the rest of the year. The access point with the best payoff for an easy walk is at the top of the Properties, a large residential development above Maple Bay Road.

Next door to St. Ann's but set well back from the road is Providence Farm. The enormous white building with a bright red roof is an unexpected sight for many coming upon it for the first time. The sign by the driveway entrance invites you to come and see what's not visible from the road, the whole village-like development behind the main building: gardens, greenhouses, planted fields, horse stables, workshops, a farm store and a small café. And always people coming and going, working in the gardens, potting plants in the nursery, mucking out the stables, shopping at the farm store, helping out in the kitchen. Providence Farm describes itself as a "horticultural therapeutic community," an organic farm operation whose work programs are designed to support those with physical and mental challenges.

Performers on stage at the 25th annual Islands Folk Festival held at Providence Farm, July 2009.

The Sisters of St. Ann, a religious order from Montreal, bought this 162-hectare (400-acre) parcel in 1864. Under the direction of its founder, Sister Mary Providence, a large building to house the first chapel and a school for girls was put up. The present building on the site has survived since 1921. The place served in various school and boarding capacities over the last century until interest and the means to keep it going petered out. In 1978 a group of community-minded people got together with a vision for how the old buildings and farm could be put to renewed use. A year later the Vancouver Island Providence Community Association came into being with the plan of turning the property into a therapeutic centre where working the land was the main treatment.

Two signs of its success are its continued expansion and its use by the entire Cowichan community. Locals come here to buy fresh produce and to volunteer in the gardens, kitchen and furniture-making shop and with the therapeutic riding association. As well, gourmet dinner and music fundraising events are often held at the farm. For more than two decades this has also been the site of the Islands Folk Festival—the second-oldest folk festival in the province—which draws thousands of people annually over a weekend in July.

A kilometre (0.6 miles) beyond Providence Farm is another of the Cowichan's oldest still-running churches. The parish of St. Peter, Quamichan, was founded in 1866, and in the church cemetery lie many of the region's earliest settlers. Among them is buried Richard Stoker, horti-culturalist and brother of Bram Stoker, the author of *Dracula*.

Maple Bay

Circling around the base of the mountain's bulk, Tzouhalem Road connects with Maple Bay Road, the route east to the salt water. Maple Bay Road, which skirts Quamichan Lake, was once thinly populated with a handful of farms sloping down to the shallow lake and a few large country estates. One such home, built in 1911, became the Quamichan Inn, a place known for its fine-dining restaurant, B&B rooms and the persistent spectre of long-gone owner Mrs. Adams.

Over the last three decades this area has been much built-up, with large residential developments advancing up the slopes in each new phase. The views are unquestionably spectacular, though local groups since the 1970s have voiced concerns over environmental impact and

Bird's eye view of Maple Bay and Bird's Eye Cove.

The beach at Maple Bay draws swimmers, paddlers, scuba divers, loungers and walkers.

the fate of Quamichan Lake. A golf course designed by Greg Norman is in the works on the upper northwest side of Mount Tzouhalem.

From the shores of Maple Bay, Saltspring Island seems but a holler away, so narrow is the intervening channel. Throughout the eastern Cowichan, but especially here on the coast, it was this proximity to the Gulf Islands that made for much trade and social intercourse (as local family trees will attest) between early settlers in the two areas. The hardy farmers who regularly rowed cattle and sheep to market in Victoria and the Lower Mainland in the early days thought nothing of crossing the narrows for an evening's dance or game of cards.

Moonrise over Maple Bay Marina, located in Bird's Eye Cove at the south end of Maple Bay.

By the 1870s Maple Bay had become, like Cowichan Bay to the south, a prominent port of entry for virtually all deliveries into the island's central region. Decades before rail or decent road access to and from Victoria existed, ships made scheduled calls to offload people, livestock, mail and every piece of machinery and bag of flour needed to keep the growing settlements going. Days when ships came in were often festive as residents from all over the area descended on Maple Bay to pick up ordered goods or send off produce.

Maple Bay's townsite was laid out in 1862, only about two years after a ferocious battle took place between two First Nations groups. It had not been uncommon for the southern Kwakiutl from up the coast on Vancouver Island to conduct summer raids on Coast Salish villages in the south, killing the men and seizing women and children to be slaves. One summer, likely in 1860, several of the Coast Salish tribes, including the Cowichan, Malahat and

The SS *Amelia* calling at Maple Bay during the town's heyday as one of the Cowichan's main commercial centres, c. 1900s. *BC Archives D-03409*

The Cowichan

Fawn lilies and shooting stars beneath the oaks at the Cowichan Garry Oak Preserve.

Saanich, joined forces to put an end to the attacks once and for all. The warriors collected in Maple Bay, hiding their canoes and readying their offensive. On the day that scouts brought news of seeing canoe-loads of Kwakiutl paddling down the island, the Salish defenders swung into action. Out into the bay they sent three of their own canoes carrying Cowichan warriors disguised as women. When the Kwakiutl came around Arbutus Point and spotted the canoes, they gave pursuit as the "women" paddled desperately back toward shore. Lured deeper into the bay, the Kwakiutl saw too late the trap that had been set. The full force of the Salish side burst from their hiding places along the shore, surrounding the enemy attackers.

The battle that followed is said to have lasted for four days. In the end every Kwakiutl warrior had been killed or drowned. Shortly afterwards, the Salish launched a series of raids on Kwakiutl settlements north near Comox and Alert Bay, defeating their enemy so soundly that no fighting occurred between the groups again.

Since then the only battles fought on water have been of a recreational boating or swimming nature. Maple Bay has long been a sailing and paddling playground and home to several marinas, a rowing club and the Maple Bay Yacht Club, started in 1925. The livestock corrals, hotel, general store and other facilities that made up the port's bustly hub are long gone. These days, "downtown" Maple Bay is a peaceful, minimally commercial seaside tickle that local residents cherish. Industry and trade headed inland to the rail line and then the highway, but you won't find anyone down by the bay who regrets that. The buzz of boats, commercial seaplanes and light marine industry in Bird's Eye Cove at the south end of the bay is just enough. All three restaurants in the village provide waterfront dining.

Past development on Maple Mountain on the bay's north side and more recent development down toward Bird's Eye Cove have changed the landscape over the years, but that's been a hard trend to stop throughout the Cowichan. The 2007 application of a private film studio to set up in a closed school in Maple Bay did stir things up a little. Nevertheless, approval was granted, and the studio—now BC's largest outside Vancouver—appears to be operating well within all the appropriate-use clauses it agreed to.

Hardy folks still regularly swim off Maple Bay's beaches in the summer. Sixty years ago some sporting events even included a swimming race from the other side of the bay back to

Cowichan Garry Oak Preserve

Just east of Quamichan Lake on the road to Maple Bay is a site that the *Vancouver Sun* has called one of the top 100 wonders of British Columbia. The Cowichan Garry Oak Preserve is regarded as one of the best examples anywhere of an intact Garry oak ecosystem.

The Garry oak is the only oak species native to BC. Its range in the province is limited almost exclusively to a narrow strip along the eastern edge of Vancouver Island and through the southern Gulf Islands—coincidentally, in the same sub-Mediterranean climate that so appeals to people and urbanization. More than 100 plant and bird species associated with the Garry oak habitat are listed in the province as "critically imperilled." For this reason Nature Conservancy Canada bought the preserve property in 1999. Its volunteers have since worked hard to keep broom at bay, encourage the spread of death camas and otherwise restore and pro-

tect the oak meadow habitat on the 22-hectare (52-acre) preserve. In the spring the meadows are at their colourful best, when camas, buttercups, violets, asters and dozens of other native wildflowers carpet the ground beneath the gnarled oaks.

The original owners of this land were the Elkingtons, who named their home and property Oak Park. The two-storey house, built in the 1890s, still stands. Heritage experts consider it to be one of the finest examples of Victorian farmhouse architecture in the Cowichan. In 2008 the house became the first one in North Cowichan to receive heritage status.

As the vulnerability of Garry oak meadows in the province is increasingly recognized, the ongoing restoration efforts of the Cowichan Garry Oak Preserve are seen as a success highlight.

SAILING RACE. MAPLE BAY REGATTA. 1.9.13. 392. Thompst

Sailing in Maple Bay is pursued as enthusiastically today (top) as it was a century ago (left).

Cowichan Valley Museum and Archives, 1990.5.3.1

the beach where the Maple Bay Rowing Club is today. The starting point was the great glacial boulder (known locally as Paddy's Mile Stone), easily seen sitting by itself just above water's edge at the bay's east end.

Genoa Bay

"A friend told me of a place like this, 'So beautiful I couldn't spit.'"

Thus wrote historian and poet Charles Lillard, not specifically about the five-kilometre (three-mile) stretch from Maple Bay to Genoa Bay, though if he'd come this way he surely would have thought it fair comment. From busy Bird's Eye Cove, the road threads its way up and into a narrow valley—a demure presence between Stoney Hill and the hulking backside of Mount Tzouhalem—passing a handful of houses and a couple of small farms. It's a picture of tranquility and tidiness, though the barn-sized rock chunks scattered in some fields point to a long-ago moment when Tzouhalem shuddered.

A strong earthquake may have rattled the conglomerate chunks loose and landslides may have brought them down. (Another theory is that erosion shifted these boulders from the upper part of the mountain to the bottom.) Cowichan elders relate vivid oral accounts about an earthquake in this area, and geologic evidence shows that the last of several major earthquakes in the Cascadia Subduction Zone occurred on January 26, 1700.

At the end of the road, the community of Genoa Bay is a tiny hooked finger of private homes and a marina, thought to be named after the home port of early settler Giovanni Baptiste Ordano. If not exactly foreign, the place does have an out-of-the-way feel. The enduring Genoa Bay Café overlooking the marina has been voted, as the sign in the parking lot

Once the site of the largest sawmill in the British Empire, Genoa Bay is now a quiet collection of homes, boats and a popular restaurant.

proclaims, "The Best Restaurant in Genoa Bay!" It's definitely that and has attracted diners for years, those only too happy for an excuse to drive the road in.

Having once hummed with the largest sawmill in the British Empire, Genoa Bay's sleepiness today is well earned. Milling began here in 1873 and continued to 1925. Trees cut at Cowichan Lake and sent downriver were collected in booms off the Cowichan estuary and floated across the water. Millions of board feet of lumber were shipped out by sailing ship and freighter to destinations around the world.

Once the mill closed for good, its 60-some buildings stood abandoned. Not until 1941 did the provincial government give the property's new owner permission to clear out the site. A large, well-appointed resort rose in its place. In 1959 this was sold to a William Morgan, who renamed it Captain Morgan's Lodge. Morgan was—or was widely believed to be—descended from the nasty (and knighted for it) privateer Sir Henry Morgan, governor of Jamaica in the 1600s. The fact that the large Canadian distiller Seagram's made a rum called Captain Morgan's only lent the lodge further pizzazz, creating an exotic if erroneous association. Overnight the newly branded lodge became *the* destination of holidayers from near and far. As G. McCurdy Gould wrote in her history of Genoa Bay, "Airplanes made scheduled trips into the bay on weekends. Launches ran from Victoria and Vancouver. Athletic young chaps were known to paddle canoes from Oak Bay to Genoa Bay for the Saturday night dances."

A fire in 1964 ended the lodge's moment in the sun. Repeated efforts to redevelop the site failed, with neither sufficient funds nor the needed consensus materializing to make possible a new hotel the size and popularity of Captain Morgan's.

View looking south over Quamichan Lake, with Duncan in the left distance and Somenos Lake to the right.

Below: Bald eagles are common across the region. The immature bald eagle shown here will develop the distinctive white head and tail feathers of a mature eagle.

Quamichan and Lakes Area

Residential streets quickly give way northeast of Duncan to low rolling hills, fields and a surprising number of lake views for an area that on the map shows only two lakes, Quamichan and Somenos. Out here horses seem to outnumber cows on any given week, even when the Avalon Equestrian Centre isn't hosting championship competitors at three-day riding events. Also near Quamichan Lake is the oldest and largest holly farm in Canada, Amblecote Estate. The slopes here have wooed grape growers as well. Alderlea Vineyards, established in 1998, is the largest in the area. Vineyard owner and winemaker Roger Dosman has used an early ripening Cabernet Sauvignon-Marechal Foch cross to make a red wine that may no less, said *WineAccess* magazine in 2008, "help define the future of Vancouver Island viticulture."

Among the more unusual residents of this area are the guests of the Pacific Northwest Raptors centre, BC's first bird of prey and falconry centre. At the centre, injured wild eagles, hawks, falcons, owls and other birds of prey are nursed back to health, and if possible, released. Others are captive-bred and trained to be flying performers. One long-time resident is Charlie, a 40-year-old bald eagle who lost a wing 35 years ago after flying into electrical power lines.

The Chemainus Valley

The Chemainus River valley is an entity unto itself. This is important to remember in conversation with local residents, some of whom feel the distinction gets overlooked when people throw the term Cowichan Valley around carelessly.

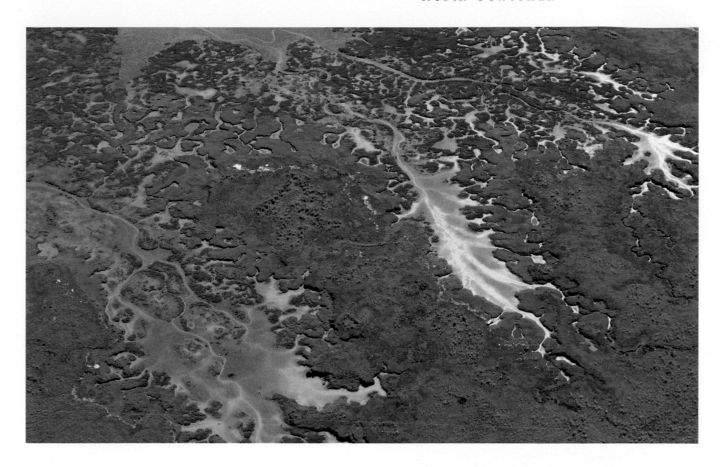

The Chemainus River rises some 50 kilometres (31 miles) northwest of Duncan in the middle of the island near Nanaimo Lakes. Its course, like that of the Cowichan River, is a channel of wild canyons and rapids, easing slowly to mellow pools and a broad, many-isleted estuary. Roosevelt elk, black bears and cougar live in the upper reaches of the valley, and coho and steelhead in the river have long attracted anglers. In the upper reaches of the valley are many mountains, but the one with particular distinction is Mount Whymper, the highest mountain in Canada (at 1,541 metres, or 5,054 feet) south of the 49th parallel. This peak is named for 19th-century English adventurer and artist Frederick Whymper, who explored Vancouver Island in the 1860s. (His brother Edward Whymper was the first climber to summit Europe's Matterhorn.) Its easy access makes Mount Whymper a popular day trip for climbers from across southern Vancouver Island.

Along with the towns of Crofton and Chemainus, two smaller communities—Westholme and Saltair—occupy the lower plain of the valley. A largely rural area, Westholme thrived during Mount Sicker's mining years, being on the way into the site from the railway and the communities of Chemainus, Crofton and Duncan. It was named for the home of C.E. Barkley, a retired captain of the Royal Navy, who was living in the area and became its first postmaster. (This Barkley's grandfather was Captain C.W. Barkley, for whom Barkley Sound was named in 1781.) Many farms continue to operate throughout Westholme today, and the Russell Farm Market on the highway is well known for its local produce.

Midway between Chemainus and Ladysmith along the ocean is the rural residential neighbourhood of Saltair, an old community that's quietly grown in recent years to about 1,800 residents. Many commute to jobs in the larger nearby centres, but going home each night to Saltair, as the name suggests, is like going home to a seaside village retreat.

Aerial view of the Chemainus estuary.

Crofton

Crofton sits on a broad, gently sloping hillside overlooking Stuart Channel and Saltspring Island and beyond to the mainland mountains. The town of 2,500 is compact, tidy and less busy than many of its neighbouring communities. Tucked in beside Maple Mountain and well away

from the highway, it feels sheltered yet ideally positioned: near enough to larger centres to satisfy work, shopping and personal needs but far enough away to remain free of traffic volume and congestion. In recent years it has undergone the kind of new growth that just about every other community in the Cowichan has, but it remains peaceful. Recent proposals for a couple of new large commercial and residential developments are neither universally supported nor universally dismissed here, but residents have made it clear they want a say in how the town evolves. BC Ferries operates a ferry between here and Vesuvius on Saltspring. This connection, combined with the ferry route between Fulford Harbour on Saltspring Island and Swartz Bay on southern Vancouver Island (the terminal nearest Victoria), creates a popular circle tour for drivers and cyclists.

For a place as peaceful and attractive as this, Crofton has endured much damning with faint praise. The reason for this is the pulp and paper mill—typically referred to as the Crofton mill no matter what company owns it—situated about 1 kilometre (0.6 miles) north of town. In 1957 British Columbia Forest Products built the mill. This bolstered the local and provincial economies, but it also made the name Crofton synonymous with pulp mill and the malodorous associations that go with what a pulp mill discharges into the air. It's "the smell of money," as the old saying goes, but it's also a smell with a serious side. In 2004 Crofton's mill hit the national news when Canadian rock singer and Saltspring Island resident Randy Bachman mounted the Clean Air Concert in Duncan to draw attention to the mill's air emissions. With a program that included Neil Young, the Barenaked Ladies and Tal Bachman, the concert raised funds to

Top: Catalyst Paper's mill at Crofton, with Saltspring Island in the background.

Above: The Old School Museum beside Crofton's waterfront includes displays about the community's smelter-town origins.

Opposite: A tug tows empty wood-chip barges northeast across Stuart Channel.

support the work of the Crofton Airshed Citizens' Group. Studies contracted by Catalyst have since shown the mill's airshed to be safe, but the Airshed Citizens' Group continues to monitor the situation.

Today, more than 50 years since the mill started up, Crofton is still sometimes pigeonholed as a mill town, though many residents work outside the community and its economic base is much more diversified than in the past. Moreover, the present mill owner, Catalyst Paper, has seen its pulp and paper operations atrophy in the last decade. In the old days the mill was a leading international supplier of kraft pulp, newsprint and directory paper. It could load more than 200 deep-sea freighters a season at its docks, sending the products worldwide. Early in 2009, after paring back shifts and employees as far as it could go, no longer able to overcome shrinking pulp markets abroad and declining fibre supplies at home, Catalyst announced a temporary closure of its pulp mill. What will happen next at the

facility, long the single-largest contributor to North Cowichan's tax base and a major employer in the region, has yet to be written.

All in all Crofton is—and isn't—what the town's namesake Henry Croft envisioned. The industrialist side of Croft likely would have approved of the mill. He did buy the land on Osborne Bay in 1900 to build a state-of-the-art copper smelter to process ore from his Mount Sicker mine. Feuding and bad blood was part of that picture too. Croft had gone head-to-head with his brother-in-law James Dunsmuir, owner of the competing Lenora copper mine and Ladysmith smelter. Croft gambled on profiting from a long, healthy run with his mine and smelter ventures. It looked like a good bet for a while. By 1902 his mine hummed and his townsite boomed, its hotels full; Victoria and Duncan newspapers extolled Crofton's brilliant future. No one expected the dream to fade so quickly, least of all Croft. He was forced to sell his plant in 1905 to the Britannia Smelting Company on the mainland, which abandoned Crofton altogether within a couple of years. After this, it was left to Croft's barely minted town to find its own way forward.

Chemainus

Like Crofton, Chemainus lies well off the highway, down along the shoreline. It's one of the oldest towns in the region, and the heritage look of many of its homes, businesses and churches points to that. So do the 40 wall-size murals painted throughout its downtown. Anyone arriving in Chemainus for the first time and knowing nothing of the town's history has only to spend half a day strolling the outdoor exhibit to get a good sense of what made this place.

The town offers more than a history lesson, however. Chemainus has become famous not only for its murals, but for its dozens of shops, galleries and cafés, and it's flourishing arts scene. Chemainus Theatre draws more than 80,000 people a year to the dramas, musicals and comedy classics it stages during its annual Chemainus Theatre Festival. Live music at the

Mural Town

Chemainus's first five murals were painted in 1982. This, combined with all the revitalization, was so successful that the town won first place in a New York sponsored competition for best downtown revitalization in North America. In the next years more murals and sculptures were commissioned, and the town began drawing several hundred thousand people each year.

In 2008 the town marked its 25th anniversary as the City of Murals and of becoming—with 39 official murals, 2 unofficial murals and a dozen sculptures—the largest outdoor art gallery in the world. The committee in charge of the project felt the time was right to move into a new chapter. Whereas the focus originally had been on portraying local history, the Festival of Murals Society voted to broaden that scope to include all of Vancouver Island. As a starting point it decided to shine the spotlight on the work of BC artist and writer Emily Carr, who travelled the island widely and painted its landscapes in the early 1900s. It's a direction that Karl, ever the visionary, fully endorses.

Chemainus's latest mural, completed in the spring of 2009, is a head-turning, brain-teasing *trompe l'oeil* work created by German artist Steffen Jünemann. The work, titled *Emily's Beloved Trees,* measures 7 by 70 metres (23 feet by 230 feet) and was the first in a series of Carr-themed paintings

The unveiling of Chemainus's first Emily Carr-inspired mural, *Emily's Beloved Trees* by Steffen Jünemann, completed in 2009.

being commissioned by the town. It is also unusual because it is the first of Chemainus's murals to be painted off-site (in this case in Jünemann's studio in Germany), shipped to Chemainus, glued onto the building wall and then finished with additional painting as necessary to complete the job. The surface that's painted on in the studio is a non-woven acrylic microfibre known as Evolon. With this new technique, outdoor murals are shown to last longer, without requiring paint and surface touch-ups, than traditional murals that are painted directly on wall surfaces.

Dancing Bean Café draws jazz, folk and other acoustic performers from all over Vancouver Island. New residential areas have expanded the town's population and reflect the vitality that's impossible to miss in this community of 4,500. A large breakwater, marina and hotel development on the waterfront is also under way, marking a new phase in the evolution of Chemainus's waterfront from industrial to residential and recreational. It's the happy outcome of what back in the late 1970s was a dire time for the town whose main employer for more than a century, the sawmill, was being shut down for good.

Chemainus became a forestry town almost the moment the first European settlers arrived in the mid-1800s. Back then the frontier settlement was known as Horseshoe Bay, after the deep U-shaped inlet it sat next to. Forestry made Chemainus. Its mill was one of the largest on the West Coast and, according to local historians, the mill site holds the record for longest continuous lumber production of anywhere in North America. In 1900 the town's Horseshoe Bay Hotel hosted not one but two American millionaires—J.D. Rockefeller and Andrew Carnegie—keen on selling their island timber holdings to the Chemainus mill.

As all the region's forestry-based communities had, Chemainus experienced many ups and downs in the business over the century of operations. Fires and market slowdowns had meant mill-worker layoffs from time to time, but mostly the town and its residents had always managed to hold on. In the late 1970s, however, severe market conditions were such that by 1979 the owner of the mill, MacMillan Bloedel, decided to close the mill completely. About 600 workers were let go. For a community whose prosperity was so dependent on the mill, the closure dealt a heavy blow. Businesses folded. Families moved away. The downtown took on a

One of Chemainus's public sculptures *In Search of Snipes,* designed and cast by Glenn Spicer in 1986.

look of neglect. Chemainus, it seemed, would be left to wither.

It was at this point that someone approached town council with an idea so nutty that even many skeptics were begrudgingly intrigued. The idea was this: First invite artists from around the world to come to the small town to paint large-format murals on downtown buildings, portraying scenes from local history. Then promote the artworks widely so that Chemainus becomes a destination for visitors from near and far, who will come to town, eat at its restaurants and shop in its galleries, clothing stores and gift shops. The man who hatched the idea was a local businessman, Karl Schutz.

The seed of this dream had taken hold in Karl's mind during a 1971 holiday in Romania, where he saw monastery towns with 400-year-old murals that depicted historic events in each community's past. Karl might never have gotten that seed to root in his world back home, however, had the ground not been roughed up by the mill's closure. Approached to help figure how to breathe life back into the town he'd lived in since 1952, Karl fired up his powers of persuasion. In 1981 he became the coordinator of a downtown revitalization project that was part of a provincially funded program. It seemed to him the right moment to push his vision of painting the town in murals. Many people felt that Karl's idea was utter nonsense, but enough others, including the young mayor at the time, Graham Bruce, became convinced there was nothing to lose by trying.

The rest, as they say, is history. Today visitors flock to Chemainus, many aboard the E&N train that stops in the heart of town. Murals and sculptures continue to be commissioned; cafés and shops are busy; the professional theatre draws performers and audiences from across BC; a hotel and numerous B&Bs offer visitors a range of accommodation options; and the summer has become a months-long festival of arts and community. In 1985, just as the mural project was picking up steam, MacMillan Bloedel opened up the mill again as a rebuilt and much modernized facility. Though its operation required a fraction of the employees needed before, its return was welcome.

The Chemainus rebirth story—"The Little Town That Did" (copyright-protected)—has been featured in articles, books and documentaries. For the premier screening of the documentary film about the project, financed in part by Karl mortgaging his home, he thought nothing of inviting Canadian historian and author Pierre Berton to be guest of honour. Berton accepted. For his unflagging enthusiasm for the project, his community and the arts in general, Karl has received a stack of provincial, national and international awards and recognition, including an honorary doctorate in 2003. Word of Chemainus's reinvention has inspired dozens of towns in five different countries to follow the "Chemainus Formula" in using the arts as a tourism generator.

Cowichan Region's Small Islands

Thetis, Kuper, Valdes and several even smaller islands that lie off Vancouver Island's east coast are also part of the Cowichan region. Although administratively under the wing of the regional district, they are often associated less with Vancouver Island and more with the Gulf Islands—a mindset that suits many residents on the small islands just fine. Ferry service operates to Thetis and Kuper from Chemainus. Access to Valdes is by private boat or floatplane only.

Common to see in the summer in Chemainus are large groups of young campers heading to or returning from the ferry dock. Two church-run camps have operated for decades on Thetis and remain well-liked destinations for children and teenagers from across BC. Thetis Island's year-round population is less than 400, but weekenders and summertime visitors can boost the number to well over 1,500. The ferry ride is only 30 minutes long, so many of the permanent residents work and shop in Chemainus. Two marinas, one on either side of Telegraph Harbour, thrum during the months of good cruising weather.

In 2006 a decommissioned Boeing 737 was sunk between Chemainus and Thetis Island to create the Xihwu artificial reef, now a big attraction for scuba divers. Notable is the large red and spiny sea urchin mask on its nose, carved in Western red cedar by Coast Salish artist Doug August. August learned to carve from his father Cicero August, a master carver and student of the celebrated carver Simon Charlie.

Kuper Island, separated from Thetis by slim Canoe Pass, is home to the Penelakut First Nation, about 560 strong. It is a community mainly of private homes, with no commercial development or services. Kuper and Thetis were originally a single land mass, joined in the middle by tidal mud flats. A passage dredged between the two islands in 1905 provides a shortcut for small boat traffic, but boaters attempting to transit "The Cut" in a vessel that's not a canoe or kayak had better hope they've read their tide charts correctly first.

Top: Sculpted sandstone formations at Pilkey Point on Thetis Island.

Above: The ferry that serves the Chemainus–Thetis Island–Kuper Island route.

7

Ladysmith and Yellow Point

At its northern end, the Cowichan Valley Regional District bumps up against and spills slightly over the 49th parallel. It's a fitting reminder of the southerliness of southern Vancouver Island relative to mainland BC. Ladysmith Harbour, formerly called Oyster Harbour, is a narrow 9-kilometre (5.6-mile) channel outfitted with everything from shoaling beaches perfect for wading and swimming to steep shoreline drop-offs perfect for accommodating keel boats and, in some parts, deep-sea freighters. Beyond the long leg of harbour are the rural communities of North Oyster and Yellow Point, together a seamlessly interconnected area of gently rolling fields and small forest stands.

In this part of the Cowichan, Nanaimo exerts a strong gravitational pull. The city of 140,000 is only

The original townsite of Ladysmith sits high on the hillside above the harbour.

15 to 20 minutes away by vehicle from the Ladysmith area, which means that many Cowichan residents work, shop and play in Nanaimo.

The original residents of the area were the Chemainus First Nation, with roots here going back about 5,000 years. Large villages existed at Kulleet Bay, Shell Beach and Coffin Point. The Chemainus (from the Hul'qumi'num word *stz'uminus*) still live along this part of eastern Vancouver Island and south to the town named after them. They operate several businesses near Ivy Green on Oyster Bay, and the Chemainus Native College and Stu"ate Lelum Secondary School are located here. At the same time the Chemainus continue to practise many age-old traditions, including fishing and shellfish harvesting. The annual war canoe races hosted by Kulleet Bay's Rainbow Canoe Club bring competitors from throughout the Pacific Northwest.

European prospectors, land agents and others on an itinerant's agenda had begun showing up around Oyster Harbour around the mid-1850s, but it wasn't until 1886 and the arrival of the E&N Railway that newcomers started arriving in greater numbers and settling in for a longer stay.

Ladysmith

Ladysmith's First Avenue sparkles during the town's month-long Festival of Lights.

In 2000 *Harrowsmith Country Life* magazine named Ladysmith one of the 10 prettiest places to live in Canada. In 2002 the town received two honours from the Heritage Society of British Columbia. And in 2003 the national Communities in Bloom organization gave Ladysmith the top award for heritage conservation for a town of its size (about 7,000). According to the Bloom judges, Ladysmith has it all: beauty, friendliness, attractive architecture and a well-

preserved history—in fact, to quote them, "so many exceptional natural resources it's hard to focus on just one."

And it's thanks to the rise and fall of several natural resource sectors that Ladysmith has undergone such an interesting metamorphosis since being established in 1904 as a coal-mining company town. Through a period of militant labour activism and then decade after decade of waxing and waning forestry-driven prosperity, Ladysmith has emerged in recent years as an attractive, stable, amenity-rich, affordable and welcoming place to live. Of course, when a place is given a name that traces its source to someone named Juana Maria de los Dolores de León—Lady Smith by marriage—perhaps a self-actualizing state of grace and sophistication is inevitable. For this propitious decision, James Dunsmuir gets the credit.

In 1900 Dunsmuir began laying out a townsite here above Oyster Bay where he'd been installing a coal port. He had decided to move his miners and their families from the collier-ies in nearby South Wellington and Extension and have them live in this bedroom community instead. The workers had no choice: Dunsmuir ordered them to move or they would lose their jobs in the mine. Most of the early miners who worked in one of Dunsmuir's four coal mines in the area had come from Europe, recruited by agents with the promise of better opportunities than the Old World offered. Much has been written about coal mining and the lot of coal miners working on Vancouver Island, elsewhere in Canada and the world. The job is considered to be one of the dirtiest, unhealthiest and most dangerous. Working hundreds of metres below the ground in a cramped, dark, humid place was the same whether it was done in a shaft in Wales, China or BC. In his book *When Coal Was King* about Ladysmith and the coal-mining industry on Vancouver Island, John R. Hinde writes in detail of the constant perils the miners faced in their "troglodytic existence":

Ladysmith coal miners heading to work, c. 1910. The town was established by James Dunsmuir in 1900, overlooking his coal port.
BC Archives E-01850

> *Explosions, rock and coal falls, and other accidents killed, maimed, and injured more workers in the coal mines than in almost any other industry. As if this were not bad enough, a miner's life was often cut short by disease, the most common of which was miner's lung, or pneumoconiosis; many also suffered physical deformities from working stooped for hours, or from their injuries.*

The actual relocation of Dunsmuir's town involved transporting, intact or in pieces, many of the existing homes, shops, churches, schools and hotels and re-erecting them within the freshly staked grid of the new town. Meanwhile, on the world stage, the British were fighting the Boer War in South Africa. When a three-month siege of British forces in the South African town of Ladysmith was finally broken, Dunsmuir commemorated the Commonwealth's collective relief by christening his Oyster Bay development with the same name. He didn't stop there. Further inspired, he named 10 of his new streets after British generals in the Boer War, among them Buller, Gatacre, Kitchener and Baden-Powell (who is, perhaps, best remembered for starting the Boy Scout movement).

The South African Ladysmith, founded in 1851, was named for Juana Maria, the Spanish wife of the Cape Colony's British governor Sir Harry Smith, and a woman much admired for her benevolent work. Lady Juana Maria Smith was a direct descendant of Juan Ponce de León, a conquistador aboard Columbus's second voyage to America and a man often connected with the legendary search for the Fountain of Youth. (Clearly "what's in a name," as it applies to Vancouver Island's Ladysmith, turns out to be a striking vein of associations.)

For the town's first two decades, coal mining and shipping dominated the economy, and the town ballooned. By 1904 there were 22 hotels and boarding houses, their clientele made up mostly of single men and business travellers. One of the latter was J.D. Rockefeller, whose Rockefeller Foundation in New York owned extensive timber rights—estimated at 500 million feet—behind the town. Also adding to Ladysmith's industrial mix for a few short years was the smelting and shipping of copper ore mined on Mount Sicker and delivered here by E&N rail.

During the early 1900s, Ladysmith's coal miners earned a reputation for being among the most militant in the province. Some of the trouble began with repeated refusal by the Dunsmuirs to acknowledge their employees' union affiliation with the United Mine Workers of America. Later, even after the Dunsmuirs were out of coal mining, discontent continued to smoulder, finally erupting into the violent Great Strike of 1912–14. Ladysmith endured riots, bombings, shootings, military occupation, hundreds of arrests and deep community divisions. A measure of the mood at the time is captured by J. Cass in *Chronicle of Ladysmith and District:*

> The strikers had met the city council in a sort of conference and in effect gave the city council notice that their functions were superseded and strikers would patrol the town and maintain what they considered suitable order. A list was drawn up of persons who were not acceptable citizens in the opinions of the strikers and a 24-hour notice was given to the undesirables to leave town under the threat of forcible removal in case of neglect to comply, and many obliged promptly.

Only the outbreak of World War I forced an end to the strike, leaving much unresolved among workers, employers and former friends.

After the demand for coal petered out in the 1930s and the collieries closed, the one-time mining town became a big-time logging and sawmilling town, which it remained until only recently. An oyster fishery that began in the early 1900s also excelled, earning Lady-smith the title "cradle of the oyster industry in British Columbia." To local resident Walter

Low tide at Transfer Beach, with the mainland's Coast Mountains in the distance.

Jones goes much of the credit for that title. Around 1912 Jones began experimenting with oyster cultivation in the harbour and discovered that the Japanese oyster (later renamed the Pacific oyster) reproduced, grew and shipped with better results than either local native or eastern American oysters did. Nine oyster operations once existed in the harbour. Today only two remain, both of which harvest their shellfish from oyster farm leases located outside Ladysmith Harbour. One of the companies, Limberis Seafood Processing, got its start in 1939 and is now one of the largest shellfish processing and purification facilities in North America.

Despite the Trans-Canada Highway running through Ladysmith, separating its downtown—uphill above the highway—from the harbourfront, the town has managed to avoid the kind of strip development that has long plagued Duncan. Nevertheless, locals remember well how tired and worn out Ladysmith had begun looking by the early 1980s. She didn't need a blousy makeover but a boost to show off her great bones to better advantage. Concerted revitalization efforts were launched, capitalizing on the place's notable assets: an old-town centre full of heritage buildings and an enviable and accessible waterfront.

Today the downtown's many old brick and stone buildings, occupied by cafés, restaurants, numerous independent retail shops, art galleries and antique stores have created an inviting environment, and the sidewalk Heritage Artifact Walk puts history into the realm of public art. The hillside setting, all the while, serves up a fortune in water views.

Ladysmith's Old Town complements the residential and commercial development that has galloped ahead at Ladysmith's south end. Much of that development accounts for the 60 percent growth in the town's population since the 1990s, growth that has occurred in spite of diminishing forestry activity in a town that once relied almost completely on it. Several new development plans now on the table—including a harbourfront proposal by a hometown girl, model and actor Pamela Anderson—indicate ongoing optimism about future growth opportunities in Ladysmith.

Art and history combine in a sculpture on First Avenue.

Bathtub racing is one of many events during the weekend-long summer celebration called Ladysmith Days.

A parade float decked out for the festivities that kick off Ladysmith's Festival of Lights. The evening's Christmas-Yuletide-solstice celebration draws thousands of spectators and participants.

On the previously industrial harbourfront are Transfer Beach Park and the island's largest open-air amphitheatre, plus the Ladysmith Maritime Museum, the Waterfront Arts Centre Gallery, marinas and a yacht club. Using both its downtown and water venues, the town hosts at least a dozen public events and festivals a year that reflect the variety of local interests. These include the OysterFeast, Vancouver Island Paddlefest and Kayak Conference, Maritime Festival, Ladysmith Days, summer music concerts, Arts on the Avenue, fall fair and—now the biggest of them all—the Festival of Lights.

Started in 1987, the Christmas-Yuletide-solstice Festival of Lights celebration has grown into the biggest event in town. On the kickoff night at the end of November, downtown streets are closed to vehicle traffic and thousands of people from the island, Lower Mainland and Sunshine Coast pour into Ladysmith for an evening of live entertainment, eating and shopping. An hour-long parade precedes the big moment when tens of thousands of lights throughout the downtown are turned on, followed then by fireworks to cap off the night.

Yellow Point

Around the north end of Ladysmith Harbour, a road off the highway wends east through the fields and forests of the communities of North Oyster and Yellow Point. Even with its proximity to Nanaimo and the Nanaimo Airport, this pocket of rural landscape feels a world away. It's a place of small farms and parks, scattered homes and artists' studios, low-key resorts and B&Bs. From the shore, for example along the beach at Blue Heron Park, there are views south and east across Stuart Channel and a succession of Gulf Islands. The honeycombed and deeply undercut sandstone ledges that extend for long stretches along this part of the coast—and which characterize Gulf Island coasts as well—are works of art wrought naturally by erosion.

Say Yellow Point in many circles and people will think "lodge" as in Yellow Point Lodge.

The reputation of the much-loved 70-year-old resort precedes it far beyond Canada. Yellow Point Lodge opened in 1939 and from day one the retreat captivated guests with its waterfront setting, romantically rustic accommodations and laid-back approach to relaxation. Today the large main lodge planted high on a sandstone rise and its beachside cabins are still commonly booked year after year by repeat guests and groups of friends who look forward to the communal meals in the dining room, reading by the nearly 3-metre-long (10-foot-long) fireplace, kayaking, swimming in the ocean or in the saltwater pool built into the rocks, and just chilling under Yellow Point's tranquilizing spell.

The resort's creator and ever-affable host, Gerry Hill, died in 1988, but made his home at the lodge until the end. Hill had been smitten by the property in 1905 as a boy, but his dream of acquiring the property took shape during his time in a prisoner-of-war camp during World War I. It was meant to be. Within a few years of buying the land, Hill moved his family on-site and set about designing, laying out and building the log lodge and small cabins. Long-time guests of the resort fondly remember the lodge's sprung dance floor, the two arbutus trees that were left to grow up through the main salon and out the roof, and the annual parties, antics and hijinks of groups that, like kids at summer camp, couldn't wait to get back each year to "the Point." This has all become part of the Yellow Point lore.

A fire in 1985 completely destroyed the lodge, but not the resort's spirit: Hill had a new lodge built on the same spot and the memorable fireplace with its 4.5-tonne (5-ton) sandstone slab of mantle still remains.

Today Richard Hill, Gerry's son, and his wife run the lodge. They recently partnered with The Land Conservancy (TLC) in a covenant that protects 26.3 hectares (65 acres) of the property, a stewardship step well in line with Gerry Hill's own attitude about preserving the forest and shoreline paradise he fell in love with more than a century ago.

The laid-back charm of Yellow Point Lodge has made it a popular destination since it opened in 1939.

8

Earth to Palate: The Cowichan Bounty

James Barber—chef, food writer and host of the long-running CBC television show *Urban Peasant*—was the first to refer to the Cowichan as "Canada's Provence." Coming from the highly respected, *gusto*-promoting Barber, the comparison has often been repeated since. Other food writers and enthusiasts have made "Napa Valley North" and "Canada's Tuscany" analogies in trying to peg the flavour and sensibility of the region. While not everyone in the Cowichan food scene is comfortable with parallels like these and the unrealistic expectations they generate, most recognize the compliment intended.

It's easy to see, however, why such comparisons originate. Along the Cowichan's eastern side is the kind of

The stock at the Fairburn Farm Cowichan Water Buffalo Dairy come from the first herd of water buffalo ever imported into Canada.

Top: Chef Mara Jernigan of Fairburn Farm Culinary Retreat and Guesthouse in Cowichan Station.
Andrei Federov

Above: Resident of the Damali Lavender Farm in Cobble Hill.

climate that supports fields of lavender, hillsides of grapevines and aspirations of olive tree and truffle growing. And there's a noticeable concentration of organic farms, small-scale specialty food producers, wineries, gourmet chefs, slow-food disciples and others of this "culinary settler" breed who have turned the Cowichan into a destination for gustatory pleasure-seekers.

In addition to Barber, key among the early wave of like-minded culinary and food-wise individuals drawn to the region were Mara Jernigan, Bill Jones and Don Genova. Jernigan, well known as a chef, instructor and past co-chair of the Vancouver Island Slow Food Convivium, has been a long-time champion of the Cowichan's bounty and has helped raise the region's gastro-profile over the last decade. At Fairburn Farm Culinary Retreat and Guesthouse in Cowichan Station, she hosts multi-course Sunday brunches in the summer as well as boot-camp cooking workshops in the winter. Jones—a chef, cookbook author and food and wine consultant—offers a wide range of cooking courses and catered dinners at his home on Deerholme Farm west of Duncan. And Genova, a writer and broadcaster with a special interest in food, lives in Cobble Hill and is actively involved in many aspects of the Cowichan's food and culinary scene.

Fairburn Farm is also known as the home of Canada's first herd of water buffalo. The 1880s farm is owned by Darrel and Anthea Archer, who took it over from Darrel's parents. The senior Archers bought Fairburn in 1954 and, way ahead of the crowd, embraced organic farming.

In 2000 Darrel and Anthea imported 19 water buffalo from Bulgaria via Denmark. They'd become intrigued by what they'd learned about the gentle nature of the animals and saw the chance to get into a specialty market: buffalo milk, the key ingredient in traditional Italian *mozzarella di bufala.* Unfortunately the bovine spongiform encephalopathy scare (BSE is also known as mad cow disease) came along. In 2002 the federal government ordered all of the Archers' original herd destroyed. A vociferous, much-publicized and far-reaching campaign to save the buffalo ensued, with the Archers and their legal counsel arguing that the stock could not have contracted the disease. Despite the protests, the Archers lost their court fight and all but their buffalo calves were put down. Post-mortem tests showed that none of the animals had been diseased.

It's taken a long time to recover, but Darrel and Anthea have rebuilt the stock. All of the milk they produce goes up-island to Comox, where Natural Pastures Cheese Company turns it into delectable balls of soft, unripened buffalo mozzarella that sell out quickly.

At feeding and milking time, Darrel moves easily among "the girls," patting their enormous heads as he goes. He and Anthea have named each one and can tell them apart even at a distance. With large black Naugahyde-like noses, bouffant-curl horns and dark-lashed eyes, the girls easily win hearts. While the Archers have moved on since 2002, a plaque by the farmhouse remains to memorialize the herd they lost.

A Revival in Growing

"Eat fresh, eat local" is both widely practised and celebrated in the Cowichan. You never have to drive far to encounter a farmers' market, organic produce store, roadside stand or year-round market garden outlet. During the year, dozens of food-focussed events occur throughout the region. The annual wine and culinary festival, chefs' dinners at Providence Farm, and special events like Cowichan Lake's Salmon and Mushroom Festival are just some examples. All are a toast to the partnering of a host of players in the region's food-savvy community.

Like Fairburn and Deerholme, several other early farms throughout the area maintain their agricultural ties. Cowichan Bay Farm, for instance, has been in the same family since

1912 and is now known primarily for organic poultry. Its owners, Lyle and Fiona Young, also opened a small-scale poultry processing business as a means of supporting their operation and other Vancouver Island poultry farms.

A somewhat different enterprise is Keating Farm Estate, a 100-year-old property near Glenora that The Land Conservancy bought in 2005 after learning of its fertile fields, heritage bat colony and architecturally unusual farmhouse. A group of shareholders now works the land as a farming co-operative, and TLC plans to restore the house and many of the outbuildings.

Then there is the growing wave of new hobby farmers to the region, individuals keen simply to own a patch of land where they can take up vegetable and flower gardening on a larger scale than is possible in an urban setting. A good case in point are food television and documentary filmmaker Nick Versteeg and his wife Elly Driessen. On a September weekend in 2005, the two joined a culinary group for a retreat at Fairburn Farm hosted by Jernigan. Being food-attuned, the Vancouver couple had heard about the Cowichan area, but they had no clear picture of what that actually meant.

It didn't take long to clue them in. As Nick recalls those memorable few days: "Mara showed us all around the Duncan and Cowichan Bay areas, introducing us to local farmers, specialty food producers and winemakers. We tasted and shopped, picked fresh vegetables from Fairburn's gardens, cooked together, ate together and talked the whole time about cooking, eating, food politics. It was fabulous."

By the time they boarded a Sunday night ferry back to the mainland, Nick and Elly were concocting a relocation plan. "We couldn't get over how beautiful the place was," Nick still enthuses. "That gorgeous countryside, the vineyards, the hobby farms and the small towns. We completely fell in love with the area." Four weeks later, they'd bought a 1.2-hectare (3-acre) property in Glenora, sold their condo and started reading up on chicken husbandry. Enticing city friends, international chefs and the Canadian Culinary Olympic team to their Laughing

Fresh produce is just part of the Cowichan's food bounty.

Geese Farm kitchen for feasting and film shoots has been no trouble. In fact "on location in Cowichan" has added a cachet they hadn't banked on.

Bounty in the Glass

In the last two decades the Cowichan has come on strong as a wine-producing region, racking up more than 12 wineries and many more vineyards to keep the winemakers supplied. The area's gravelly soils, warm, dry summers and mild, wet winters create growing conditions often likened to those of northern France and Germany. Among the main grape varieties grown here are Ortega, Siegerrebe, Pinot Gris, Pinot Noir and Marechal Foch. Several wineries also use berries, most commonly blackberries, to make award-winning port-style dessert wines.

Merridale Ciderworks in Cobble Hill is Canada's largest producer of craft ciders made from cider apples. Its owners, Janet Docherty and Rick Pipes, bought the orchard and small cidery in 2000 and have since expanded it in every way—not bad, Rick says, for two city people with no previous agricultural background. In addition to growing and harvesting their own apples on 5 hectares (13 acres), producing 8 different types of ciders, running a tasting room, and hosting tours and special events, they built and operate a large bistro. In 2007 they added the Brandihouse, a new building to accommodate the 200-litre (52-gallon) Mueller handcrafted still they bought in Germany. From the gleaming copper and stainless steel machine, as beautiful to look at as it is functional, they are producing fortified dessert ciders and Calvados-style brandies from their own apples and local berries. As Rick sees it, the still nicely rounds out Merridale's use of the orchard's resources, with the apple pomace (the solid remains left over after the cider-making pressings) now being fermented and distilled into the clear fruit spirit known as an *eau-de-vie*.

Bounty on the Fork

According to Economic Development Cowichan, the region supports more than 690 farms, a quarter of the total number on Vancouver Island. What's going to market from those farms adds up to a long and varied list. A short sample: milk and eggs, beef and lamb, pork and poultry, gourmet greens and asparagus, Saskatoons and cranberries, honey and hazelnuts, emu meat and fallow venison. A resurgence in "backyard" grain-growing has also begun in the region, with particular interest going into the less hybridized grain varieties, including red fife, quinoa, emmer, Kamut and spelt.

Rich yields come from the wild too. In the spring, sap is tapped from the bigleaf maple and turned into syrup. Blackberries are a summertime abundance. In the fall, more than 30 kinds of edible mushroom can be found growing wild in the region—chanterelles, shaggy manes, boleti and pine mushrooms to name a few. Guided mushroom hunt-cook-eat day or weekend outings are offered throughout the Cowichan region. The Aerie Resort on the Malahat has become known on the island for hosting mushroom foraging excursions led by resort neighbour and Benedictine monk, Brother Michael.

Specialty food producers, like the wine and cider producers, have attracted much attention. One example is True Grain Bread and Mill in Cowichan Bay. It was started by Jonathan Knight, who was among the first of a new wave of fresh-food businesses to move into Cowichan Bay. In 2008 Knight passed the baguette to new owners Bruce and Leslie Stewart, who are carrying on with the winning formula of milling and grinding grains to handcraft organic breads.

Another standout is Hilary's Cheese Company. In 1992, when Hilary and Patty Abbott moved from Ottawa to the Cowichan, it was not to make cheese. However, six years later the call of the vat and pasteurizer was too great to resist. A decade later they're turning out a range of cow and goat cheeses weekly to keep up with demand and aiming to double production in the next few years.

Farmers' markets, retail shops and farm-gate stands carry the Cowichan's fresh produce and specialty food and wine products.

At Venturi-Schulze Vineyards, Giordano Venturi and Marilyn Schulze produce not just superb wines from their organic grapes but superb balsamic vinegar made according to traditional methods that involve a complicated, years-long process. When Giordano came to Canada from his hometown near Modena, Italy, he brought with him a portion of his family's original vinegar barrel begun in 1970. That became the mother, or starter, from whence all of Venturi-Schulze's vinegar barrels have since sprung.

All of this revived interest in local, organic, small-scale food production takes full advantage of the Cowichan's favourable soils and climate, as well as of the legacy left by early farmers whose back-breaking labours created fields out of dense forest. The many community-wide agricultural initiatives today not only bring residents together but the combined effect has brought a focus to the area's own distinct cuisine. As Rick Pipes of Merridale Ciderworks puts it, "When people travel, they want to be able to try the food and drink that is rooted in the region they're in; they want to learn more about the place by sampling what is grown, raised, harvested and made there. Here in the Cowichan we're able to give people that experience now, a real taste of what the region has to offer."

9

Exploring the Region

Whether you visit the Cowichan for a day or for a week, there's a good chance you'll wish you had planned for a longer stay.

For those interested in outdoor pursuits and exploration, the could-do list is long and includes: cycle touring, mountain biking, day hiking and backcountry hiking, fishing, golfing, canoeing, swimming, tubing, horseback riding, birdwatching, waterskiing, ocean and river (whitewater) kayaking, windsurfing and kiteboarding, sailing, scuba diving, paragliding and camping (backpacking and drive-in). For those interested in arts, culture, history, good food and shopping, there are just as many could-dos throughout the region, from attending live music and theatre to visiting museums, galleries and artists' studios to sampling the region's food and wine at its dozens of wineries, specialty food shops, farmers' markets, cafés and restaurants.

The information here, along with the contact information, will help you with planning your first or next trip to the region.

Getting to the Cowichan

Getting to the Cowichan requires first getting to Vancouver Island:

By water: From the BC mainland, BC Ferries' three main routes to the south island and mid-island are: Tsawwassen to Victoria (Swartz Bay), Tsawwassen to

Kayaking in the early evening in Cowichan Bay.

Competitors in Brentwood College's annual international rowing regatta.

Nanaimo (Duke Point, near Nanaimo) and Horseshoe Bay (West Vancouver) to Nanaimo (Departure Bay). Other options with BC Ferries include Powell River to Courtenay-Comox, Saltspring Island to Crofton, and Brentwood Bay (Saanich Peninsula) to Mill Bay.

From Washington State, the three ferry routes to Vancouver Island are: Anacortes to Sidney (Saanich Peninsula), Port Angeles to Victoria, and Seattle to Victoria (aboard the high-speed Victoria Clipper ferries, foot passenger only).

Visitors arriving by private boat can find moorage and other marine services at the many marinas located along the Cowichan coastline, including at Ladysmith, Thetis Island, Chemainus, Crofton, Maple Bay, Genoa Bay, Cowichan Bay, Cherry Point and Mill Bay.

By air: Commercial airlines operate out of Victoria International Airport (located on the Saanich Peninsula) and Nanaimo Airport (located in Cassidy, just north of Ladysmith). Several floatplane companies also offer a number of flights daily between Vancouver and downtown Nanaimo and between Vancouver and Maple Bay. These companies offer charter flight services as well.

Once you're on the island, getting to the Cowichan is straightforward:

By road: From both Nanaimo and Victoria, the Trans-Canada Highway is the main route along the east side of the island. Intersecting with the highway are the many main and secondary roads that lead to the Cowichan's oceanside and inland communities and backcountry areas. The main road to Lake Cowichan is Highway 18. There's also daily bus service from Nanaimo and Victoria to a number of the main towns in the region. As well, the E&N train, operated by VIA Rail, makes several scheduled Cowichan stops on its one up-island and one down-island run a day.

Accommodation

The Cowichan region offers a wide choice of accommodation to suit a range of needs, occasions, seasons and budgets, from a Relais & Châteaux mountainside resort (The Aerie Resort and Spa on the Malahat) to dozens of hotels, motels, inns, lodges, guest houses, B&Bs, house-boats, campgrounds and vacation rentals (houses, condos, apartments and cabins). Many places also feature seasonal and special packages with, for example, a golf, fishing, kayaking, diving, winery tour, culinary or professional theatre focus.

Seasonal Sampler

There are too many cultural and arts festivals, farmers' markets, regattas and fairs throughout the region to list here. Check the community calendar of events online (see contact information on page 140). Here are just a few suggestions to help you find seasonal events that match the time of your visit:

Pre-spring/Spring:
– attend the Cowichan International Aboriginal Festival of Film and Art
– sample the goods at the Bigleaf Maple Syrup Festival at the BC Discovery Forest Centre
– stroll the Cowichan Garry Oak Preserve near Maple Bay, Mayo Creek Gardens and the Memorial Rhododendron Park near Lake Cowichan, or the long-running Mill Bay Garden Club's flower and garden show, or take the annual Ladysmith garden tour
– watch the rowing action at the Brentwood College Regatta
– walk the docks at Maple Bay Marina to see the Maple Bay Wooden Boat Festival
– take in the Vancouver Island PaddleFest and Kayak Conference at Transfer Beach in Ladysmith

Summer:
– play a round of golf at one of the region's five golf courses
– visit the region's many wineries or its estate cidery for a tasting and a meal
– take in the two-week-long Duncan-Cowichan Summer Festival
– tube down the Cowichan River
– swim at Lake Cowichan or in the Cowichan or Chemainus Rivers, or for a saltwater taste, at the beach at Bamberton, Maple Bay, Ladysmith or Yellow Point
– attend the weekend-long Islands Folk Festival at Providence Farm

Late summer/Fall:
– attend the weekend-long Cowichan Exhibition agricultural fair
– walk or run in the Great Lake Walk and Ultramarathon around Cowichan Lake
– give yourself over to the gustatory weekend-long Wine and Culinary Festival

Late fall/Winter:
– sample the goods at Lake Cowichan's Salmon and Mushroom Festival
– sign up for a mushroom hunting and cooking class
– visit the Yellow Point Cranberry Farm and stock up on all manner of cranberry treats
– spend the evening at the Ladysmith Festival of Lights

The beauty of the local harvest.

Year-round:
- cycle the Trans Canada Trail, being sure to visit the Kinsol Trestle, which lies between the Shawnigan Lake and Glenora part of the route
- go on a guided kayaking or nature-watching cruise from Cowichan Bay or Ladysmith
- take a walking tour of Duncan's totems, Chemainus's murals or Ladysmith's heritage buildings and artifacts
- plan a full-day shopping tour of the region's many independent specialty shops and boutiques

Community Sampler

Every community offers more than can be listed here. Check the contact information provided on page 140 for details. Here are a few suggestions:

South Cowichan
- visit downtown Cobble Hill's shops and nearby Merridale Ciderworks for lunch, dinner or a spa treatment
- in downtown Shawnigan Lake, visit the Shawnigan Lake Museum and then check out the notable shops and restaurants nearby
- walk or cycle along the Trans Canada Trail to see the Kinsol Trestle
- swim, fish or canoe at West Shawnigan Lake Provincial Park
- visit the Cowichan Bay Maritime Centre as well as the village's many shops, galleries, cafés and restaurants

Duncan and Vicinity
- spend a day in downtown Duncan seeing the totems, touring the Quw'utsun' Cultural Centre and the Cowichan Valley Museum in the heritage train station, and visiting the many shops, galleries, cafés and restaurants
- stop at Whippletree Junction on the highway to browse its collection of independent shops
- walk the Cowichan River Footpath through Cowichan River Provincial Park
- catch live music at the Duncan Garage Showroom, open nearly every night of the week
- birdwatch at the Somenos Marsh Conservation Area
- visit the BC Forest Discovery Centre

Celebrate the year's local bounty at Cherry Point Vineyards during the Cowichan's annual Wine and Culinary Festival.

The Cowichan Lake Area and Westward
- drive and walk up Mount Prevost to see the memorial tower and big valley views
- visit the Kaatza Station Museum in Lake Cowichan and the shops and cafés downtown
- drive around Cowichan Lake to visit its small communities and see the lake and mountain views
- head out west of the lake to Carmanah Walbran Provincial Park and Nitinat Lake, or pick up the Pacific Marine Circle Tour from Mesachie Lake to Port Renfrew on the island's west coast

North Cowichan
- visit Providence Farm to see the gardens, buy fresh produce or attend a dinner or music event
- do a short or a long hike on Mount Tzouhalem and get a bird's-eye view of the Cowichan estuary and the Cowichan River valley

Water park fun at Transfer Beach in Ladysmith.

– watch flying demonstrations at the Pacific Northwest Raptors centre near Quamichan Lake
– drive or cycle the bucolic "lake district" in and around Quamichan and Somenos lakes
– stroll the Sea Walk in Crofton
– visit Chemainus River Provincial Park
– spend a day touring Chemainus to see its murals, the Chemainus Valley Museum and its many shops, galleries, cafés and restaurants
– attend a matinee or evening performance at the Chemainus Theatre
– take the ferry to Thetis Island from Chemainus for a day visit or overnight stay

Ladysmith and Yellow Point
– spend a day touring Ladysmith's Old Town and visiting its many shops, galleries, cafés and restaurants as well as the Ladysmith Maritime Museum
– go kayaking in Ladysmith Harbour, walking in Holland Creek Trail or hiking up to Heart Lake
– take in Ladysmith's annual summertime Arts on the Avenue festival and its late November Festival of Lights
– explore the beach at Blue Heron Park on Yellow Point

CONTACTS FOR FURTHER INFORMATION

Transportation

BC Ferries: 1-888-BCFERRY (223-3779) or (250) 386-3431; www.bcferries.com

Coho Ferries: Blackball Transport operates the Coho Ferry between Port Angeles, WA and Victoria: (250) 386-2202; www.cohoferry.com

Victoria Clipper: Clipper Navigation operates between Seattle and Victoria: (250) 382-8100 or 1-800-888-2535; www.victoriaclipper.com

Washington State Ferries: Anacortes to Sidney, BC (206) 464-6400; www.wsdot.wa.gov/Ferries/Schedule

VIA Rail: 1-888-842-7245; www.viarail.ca

Harbour Air: 1-800-665-0212; www.harbour-air.com

Saltspring Air: 1-877-537-9880; www.saltspringair.com

Tourism and Visitor Services in the Cowichan

Tourism Cowichan: 1-888-303-3337; www.tourismcowichan.com

Chemainus & District Chamber of Commerce & Visitor Centre: (250) 246-3944; www.chemainus.bc.ca

Cowichan Lake District Chamber of Commerce & Visitor Centre: (250) 749-3244; www.cowichanlake.ca

Duncan-Cowichan District Chamber of Commerce & Visitor Centre: 1-888-303-3337 or (250) 746-4636 ; www.duncancc.bc.ca

Ladysmith Chamber of Commerce & Visitor Booth: (250) 245-2112; www.ladysmithcofc.com

South Cowichan Chamber of Commerce & Visitor Booth: (250) 743-3566; www.southcowichanchamber.org

Tourism Vancouver Island: (250) 754-3500; www.vancouverisland.travel

BC Parks (for information on parks, campgrounds and trails operated by BC Parks): www.env.gov.bc.ca/bcparks/

Nature Cowichan (for information about local hiking areas, trails and outdoor events): www.naturecowichan.net

Small Sample of Accommodation

The Aerie Resort and Spa: 1-800-518-1933 or (250) 743-7115; www.aerie.ca

The Quamichan Inn: (250) 746-7028; www.thequamichaninn.com

Sahtlam Lodge and Cabins: (877) 748-7738; www.sahtlamlodge.com

Yellow Point Lodge: (250) 245-7422; www.yellowpointlodge.com

BC Parks (campground information and bookings): www.env.gov.bc.ca/bcparks

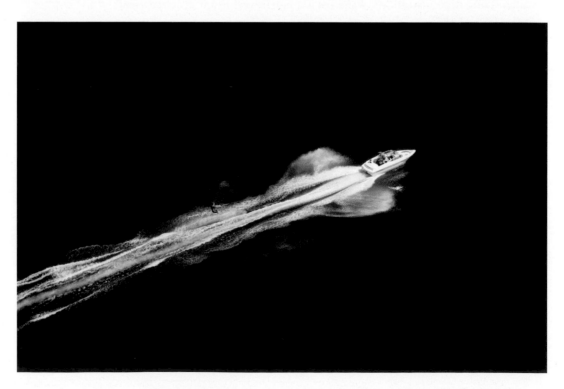

Waterskiing is a popular activity on hot days at Shawnigan Lake.

SELECTED SOURCES AND FURTHER READING

Backroad Mapbooks. *Fishing Mapbook: Region—Vancouver Island*. Burnaby, BC: Mussio Ventures, 2008.

Blier, Richard K. *Hiking Trails I: South-Central Vancouver Island and the Gulf Islands*. Victoria: Orca Book Publishers, 2000.

Bonner, Virginia. *The Hamlet with an Attitude, 1886–1945: The Story of Cobble Hill Village*. Duncan, BC: Firgrove Publishing, 2001.

Bowen, Lynne. *Boss Whistle: The Coal Miners of Vancouver Island Remember*. Lantzville, BC: Oolichan Books, 1982.

Bowen, Lynne. *Those Lake People: Stories of Cowichan Lake*. Vancouver: Douglas & McIntyre, 1995.

Dash, Donna. *Mural Magic: Karl Schutz and Chemainus, "The Little Town That Did."* Chemainus, BC: Mural Magic Publications, 2006.

Dougan, Robert I. *Cowichan My Valley*. Cobble Hill, BC: by the author, 1973.

Ellis, Adelaide. *Along Mill Bay Road*. Mill Bay, BC: by the author, 1990.

Gibson, Alice L. *Green Branches and Fallen Leaves: The Story of a Community, Shawnigan Lake 1887–1967*. Shawnigan Lake, BC: Shawnigan Lake Confederation Centennial Celebrations Committee, 1967; reprint 1976, 1980, 1986.

Goodacre, Richard. *Dunsmuir's Dream: Ladysmith—The First Fifty Years*. Victoria: Porcepic Books, 1991.

Gould, G. McC. *Genoa Bay Reckonings*. Genoa Bay, BC: Lambrecht Publication, 1st ed. c. 1977.

Henry, Tom. *Small City in a Big Valley: The Story of Duncan*. Madeira Park, BC: Harbour Publishing, 1999.

Hinde, John. *When Coal Was King: Ladysmith and the Coal-Mining Industry on Vancouver Island*. Vancouver: UBC Press, 2003.

Hodding, Bruce. *North Cowichan: A History in Photographs*. North Cowichan, BC: Corporation of District of North Cowichan, BC, 1998.

Kimantas, John. *The Essential Vancouver Island Outdoor Recreation Guide*. North Vancouver: Whitecap Books, 2008.

Ladysmith Centennial Core Committee and Take 5 (541806 BC Ltd). *Ladysmith: 100 Years, 1904–2004*. Ladysmith, BC: 2004.

McCrimmon, Marilyn. *Custodian of Yellow Point: The Biography of Gerry Hill*. Victoria: Beach Holme Publishers, 1991.

Mackay, Ellen. *Places of Worship in the Cowichan and Chemainus Valleys*. Victoria: Sono Nis Press, 1991.

Marshall, Daniel P. *Those Who Fell from the Sky: A History of the Cowichan Peoples*. Duncan, BC: Cowichan Tribes, Cultural and Education Centre, 1999.

Mayo, Joan. *Paldi Remembered: 50 Years in the Life of a Vancouver Island Logging Town*. Duncan, BC: Paldi History Committee, 1997.

Norcross, E. Blanche. *The Warm Land: A History of Cowichan*. Duncan, BC: Island Books, first published 1959; rev. ed. 1975.

Olsen, W.H. *Water Over the Wheel: A Story of Danger, Mystery, Heartbreak and Success—the Chemainus Valley*. Chemainus, BC: Karl Schutz and the Chemainus, Crofton and District Chamber of Commerce, 2nd ed. 1981.

Our Favourite Hikes in the Cowichan Lake Area. Lake Cowichan, BC: Community Economic Adjustment Committee, 2003.

Paterson, T.W. *Cowichan Chronicles*. Duncan, BC: Firgrove Publishing, Vol. 1, 2001; Vol. 2, 2004; Vol. 3, 2006; Vol. 4, 2008.

Paterson, T.W. *Riches to Ruin: The Boom to Bust Saga of Vancouver Island's Greatest Copper Mine*. Duncan, BC: Firgrove Publishing, 2007.

Pojar, Jim, and Andy MacKinnon, compil. and eds. *Plants of Coastal British Columbia: Including Washington, Oregon and Alaska*. Vancouver: Lone Pine Publications, 1994.

Reid, D.C. *Vancouver Island Fishing Guide*. Portland: Frank Amato Publications, 2008.

Saywell, John F.T. *Kaatza: The Chronicles of Cowichan Lake*. Lake Cowichan, BC: The Cowichan Lake District Centennial Committee, 1st ed. 1967.

Thom, Ian. *E. J. Hughes*. Vancouver: Douglas & McIntyre, 2002.

Turner, Robert D. *Vancouver Island Railroads*. Winlaw, BC: Sono Nis Press, 1997.

Yorath, Chris. *The Geology of Southern Vancouver Island*. Madeira Park, BC: Harbour Publishing, 2005.

AUTHOR'S NOTE

By almost any measure I am a newcomer to the Cowichan, having moved here in August 2007. Thus I do not have generations, a lifetime or even decades of Cowichan experience. No local road, cove or business is named for a great-relative of mine. And I've got no memory of what life was like when logging, milling and other forestry operations held court in virtually every corner of the Cowichan. Nevertheless, shortly after my arrival to the region, when photographer Kevin Oke invited me to collaborate on producing a book for Harbour Publishing about the Cowichan, I jumped at the opportunity. No better outlet could I have imagined for sharing with the wider world my enthusiasm for everything I was, and still am, discovering about this place.

My sincere thanks to Kevin and to all in the region, too numerous to mention individually, who made time to meet with me or take calls to answer questions, recommend books and other reference materials, and share their insights about the Cowichan. Special thanks to Kathryn Gagnon, curator of the Cowichan Valley Museum, and Dave Moss, long-time Cowichan resident and volunteer at the museum's archives, who both read and commented on an early draft of the manuscript. Others whose historical knowledge of the Cowichan was of great help include T.W. Paterson, Lori Treloar (curator of the Shawnigan Lake Museum) and Karl Schutz. Cherie Oke offered welcome input about local flora. My appreciation also to all friends and family who shared the thrill of the exploration with me on the ground and endured a year-and-a-half's worth of steady assault by short history lesson, astonishing fact and riveting trivia. Especially supportive through it all were, as ever, Lawrence and Naomi.

Finally, I am indebted to Susan Mayse, my editor, whose keen eye, inquiring mind and impressive knowledge about so many things improved this text enormously.

PHOTOGRAPHER'S NOTE

Many assisted me in my quest for images of the Cowichan region. While there are far too many to mention individually, thanks to those who allowed me to photograph them while they went about their business and pleasure. Thanks are due, also, to the many friends and family who accompanied me on various excursions, contributing companionship, laughter, great food and often subject material for the photos. Special thanks to friend and author Georgina Montgomery, to her husband Lawrence Pitt and to my wife and constant supporter Cherie Oke.

Notes about the Photography

The Cowichan Valley is a photographer's dream. Countless festivals and events, scenery ranging from ocean beaches to raging rivers and stunning mountains, all mixed with a fascinating history of cultures and entrepreneurial pursuits—it doesn't get much better than that.

I'm often asked what type of equipment I use and what my digital workflow entails. The photographs in this book were shot with a Nikon D2X and a Nikon D300. At 12.4 and 12.3 megapixels respectively, these cameras provide detail in images that was impossible only a few years ago. The lenses I used ranged from an extremely wide-angle 10mm to long telephotos of 300mm and every focal length in between.

Projects like this are a huge undertaking for a photographer, not just in the sheer number of images produced (in this case approximately 40,000) but also in the image processing and cataloguing efforts. The images were photographed in the proprietary Nikon raw format NEF. These raw images were processed using Nikon NX2 software that provides incredible control over the final image. If further additional work was required to refine the image, I used Photoshop CS4. Labelling and keywording were done in Photo Mechanic—a very versatile software program—and catalogued using Extensis Portfolio. Photography accounts for only about 20 percent of the time I spent working on this project; the remaining 80 percent was spent in long hours at the computer editing images, adding keywords, accurately captioning the images and making final selections for the book.

Two years of shooting and countless stories later, these final images represent a small cross-section of this stunningly beautiful area. Throughout my travels, I met dozens of wonderful people, visited the many small towns and villages, hiked hundreds of kilometres of trails and sampled the varied culinary delights this area has to offer. I'm delighted to call the Cowichan region home and hope you enjoy this personal view of it as much as I enjoyed my photographic journey.

For additional information and photographs, please visit my website: www.cowichanvalleyphotos.com.

To Lawrence. — G.M.
For my wife, Cherie. — K.O.

Harbour Publishing Co. Ltd.
P.O. Box 219, Madeira Park, BC, V0N 2H0
www.harbourpublishing.com

All photographs by Kevin Oke unless stated otherwise
Edited by Susan Mayse
Maps by Roger Handling
Cover design by Anna Comfort
Text design by Roger Handling
Printed on 10% PCW recycled stock
Printed and bound in Canada

Harbour Publishing acknowledges financial support from the Government of Canada through the Book Publishing Industry Development Program and the Canada Council for the Arts, and from the Province of British Columbia through the BC Arts Council and the Book Publishing Tax Credit.

Library and Archives Canada Cataloguing in Publication

Montgomery, Georgina
The Cowichan : Duncan, Chemainus, Ladysmith and region / written by Georgina Montgomery ; photos by Kevin Oke.

Includes index.
ISBN 978-1-55017-490-8

1. Cowichan Valley (B.C.). 2. Cowichan Valley (B.C.)—Pictorial works.
I. Oke, Kevin, 1958- II. Title.

FC3845.C68M65 2009   971.1'2   C2009-903470-0